"They say I'm not a girl"

"They say I'm not a girl"

Case Studies of Gender Verification in Elite Sports

MAX DOHLE

McFarland & Company, Inc., Publishers

Jefferson, North Carolina

LIBRARY OF CONGRESS CATALOGUING-IN-PUBLICATION DATA

Names: Dohle, Max, author.
Title: They say I'm not a girl : case studies of gender verification in elite sports
Description: Jefferson, North Carolina : McFarland & Company, Inc.,
Publishers, 2020 | Includes bibliographical references and index.
Identifiers: LCCN 2020024478 | ISBN 9781476673783 (paperback : acid free paper) ∞
ISBN 9781476637013 (ebook)
Subjects: LCSH: Sports—Sex differences. | Sex discrimination
in sports. | Intersex athletes.
Classification: LCC GV708.8 .D64 2020 | DDC 306.483—dc23
LC record available at https://lccn.loc.gov/2020024478

BRITISH LIBRARY CATALOGUING DATA ARE AVAILABLE

ISBN (print) 978-1-4766-7378-3
ISBN (ebook) 978-1-4766-3701-3

On the cover: Dutee Chand at the 2017 Asian Athletics Championships
(Athletics Federation of India)

Printed in the United States of America

McFarland & Company, Inc., Publishers
Box 611, Jefferson, North Carolina 28640
www.mcfarlandpub.com

Table of Contents

orandum est ut sit mens sana in corpore sano.
fortem posce animum mortis terrore carentem,
qui spatium vitae extremum inter munera ponat
naturae, qui ferre queat quoscumque labores,
nesciat irasci, cupiat nihil et potiores
Herculis aerumnas credat saevosque labores
et venere et cenis et pluma Sardanapalli.
monstro quod ipse tibi possis dare; semita certe
tranquillae per virtutem

—Juvenal, Satire X

You should pray for a healthy mind in a healthy body.
Ask for a stout heart that has no fear of death,
and deems length of days the least of Nature's gifts,
that can endure any kind of toil,
that knows neither wrath nor desire and thinks
the woes and hard labors of Hercules better than
the loves and banquets and downy cushions of Sardanapalus.
What I commend to you, you can give to yourself;
for assuredly, the only road to a life of peace is virtue.

Preface

The Humiliating Practice of Gender Verification

"They say I'm not a girl," replied Foekje Dillema when her teammates asked her what had happened after she was taken off the train in July 1950 by board members of the Dutch Athletic Union. Dillema had been questioned because she did not participate in a mandatory gender verification for the 1950 European Athletics Championships to be held in Brussels in August. Right there on the railway platform, Dillema was suspended from the track for life. She lost all her records and her national title on the 200-meter sprint and never ran again in an elite competition after this incident.[1]

She was allowed back on the train, but only to collect her suitcase, leaving the other girls in bewilderment. Back on the platform she watched the train carry her teammates to an international match in France. She travelled back home and didn't leave her house for over a year. Dillema was the first victim of a mandatory gender verification instituted by the International Amateur Athletic Federation (IAAF). All athletes in the female competition were required to bring a gender certificate to the European Championships in Brussels on August 23, 1950.

For sixty years nobody knew why this Dutch sprinter had been barred. There was the usual conspiracy theory, of course. But the real reason became apparent after she died in 2007: a DNA test on skin cells taken from her clothing revealed she was intersex. You will find her life story, and other biographies of suspended intersex athletes, in this book. Stories will cover the athletes' lives, from the cradle to the disqualification, and the "after" life. And yes, sometimes even back to the time before they were born.

Suspending athletes was and is not unusual, of course. Athletes are banned for lots of reasons: misbehavior, doping, drinking, and sometimes because of ethnicity, religion or just who they are. The Nazis suspended Gretel Bergmann because she was Jewish; the chairman of the American Olympic Committee Avery Brundage put the Jewish relay runners Stoller and Glickman aside in 1936 because he did not want to offend "Herr Hitler." He also suspended Eleonor Holm for spending the night at the ship's bar. And women were barred simply for their gender.

In 80 years of gender testing no male fraud (males posing deliberately as females in order to enter the women's competition) was ever detected. But the by-catch were dozens of intersex athletes. This book is about the intersex athletes who were suspended for having a presumed unfair benefit from a disorder of sexual development. They took part in elite competition as females.

In most sports there is a segregated male and female competitive field. That is not a goal in itself; the intention is to create a level playing field. In athletics, for instance, men perform, overall, 12 percent better than women.[2] Separation of the sexes makes elite sports possible for women. They wouldn't stand a chance against men, with rare exceptions. The female competition used to be protected by unwritten rules. The federations decided ad hoc who was allowed to start and who wasn't.

Nature doesn't always divide the sexes into two clear categories. It is estimated that about one in 100 humans is intersex, falling somewhere in between the two scale ends of man and woman.[3] The athletes in this book were assigned female at birth, and they felt themselves to be girls. They were raised as female and did not feel like they were born "in the wrong body" (as transgender people do). Their core gender is female, but they have physical characteristics of both sexes. In most cases this consists of a vagina in combination with small, internal, infertile testes. But the testes still produce limited amounts of male hormones. Therefore, the athletes are called hyperandrogenic, meaning that the testosterone level in their blood is higher than that of a typical woman. This condition is sometimes only revealed after a gender verification test. The athletes were always shocked by the outcome of this examination. They had never expected to be intersex. On top of this traumatic shock they were suspended for life.

As of 1936, intersex athletes were banned from competition. Some were able to fight back and regained their ability to compete with other females. But most women never returned to competition. They lost their formal right to play sports. But they of course have a moral right to take part in competition. In my opinion all people should have the right to participate in sports. Unless they cheat. But intersex athletes never intended to distort the competition. They are not frauds.

The Olympic movement hammers on the slogan that taking part is more important than winning. For intersex individuals, winning could be worse than taking part. They had to leave the arena through the back door, often with a lifelong stigma of being called man-woman, cheater or hermaphrodite, or even worse. The Olympic movement uses fine rhetoric, but has never embraced *all* athletes that played by the rules. The intersex athlete has always been a problem for the IOC, rather than a challenge to be faced and dealt with fairly. Intersex athletes are looked upon as frauds, not as human beings who have a right to compete. It's easier to get rid of frauds than human beings. Intersex athletes don't know anything is wrong with them until a doctor tells them there was something terribly wrong with their chromosomes and hormones. This always comes as a shock.

In 2001, a 19-year-old athlete from India committed suicide after a disturbing phone call about her gender verification. She hung up in tears, tied bags with stones to her ankles, jumped into the deep village well and drowned. The suicide was an all-time low of the history of gender testing. The girl was probably blackmailed by someone who had seen the outcome of her gender verification.[4] That has always been one of the main problems of sex testing: the IAAF and the IOC could not or did not respect the privacy of the women concerned.

Was there no protest against the treatment of intersex athletes? Yes, there were protests—from scientists, from human rights organizations, even from governments. Nelson Mandela stood behind 800-meter runner Caster Semenya all the way. But even Mandela could not stop the travesty in Semenya's case. International sports federations believe they operate above national laws and can make their own moral arguments not hindered by knowledge or empathy.

This book is not always an easy one, but it is a necessary book. It covers the dark side of elite sports. It is a book which intends to change negative opinions about and the humiliations of intersex athletes. It intends to refute pseudo-scientific arguments—even ones made by scientists—and to unmask prejudices on intersex conditions.

Banning intersex athletes from competing is humiliating and should stop, without any conditions. Intersex women have a right to compete in elite competitions. Born and raised as girls and officially women, they belong in the female competitive sphere.

3

Preface

These women were banned without any solid arguments. Before 2018 no research had been done on the effects on athletic performance caused by high natural testosterone levels.[5] But scientists and major sports federations have always assumed that intersex athletes were competing unfairly. The question, however, is not just a scientific one, it is also on the moral values we want to uphold. About including all athletes in the Olympic movement. Being part of the movement should be more important than winning or losing.

This is a book about the lives of suspended athletes: Who were they? Why were they suspended? How were they barred? What effect did the disqualification have on their private lives? It is sports history, as well as a book about moral values, but above all it is a book about real people who were not allowed to do what they did best and liked best: compete in elite sports.

Preliminaries

The Man-Woman Athlete in the 1930s;
or, Gender Reassignment in Pre-War Sport

Witold Smętek was born Zofia Smętek on December 17, 1910, in Kalisz in Poland. Twenty-seven years later Zofia underwent sex reassignment and became Witold. Before this series of operations Zofia was a multi-talented sportswoman: an elite runner, a javelin thrower, cyclist and even the Polish national table tennis champion. On top of it all Zofia bacame the national cross-country champion in 1932.

She was primarily a javelin thrower. Zofia participated in international championships in Europe and in Japan. In Poland she won a gold medal, but on the international stage, she was just not good enough for a medal. Mostly she came in fourth or fifth. In those days javelin throwing was a two-handed sport—not at the same time, of course. Athletes had to throw three times with the right hand and three times with the left. The best scores from each hand were added together. In the finals, three finalists could throw with their favorite hand. In 1932 Zofia threw a new world record in Hazenie, Poland. Zofia then became a celebrity in Poland.

"Due to her physical beauty" she was presumed to be a girl at birth. Zofia probably had ambiguous sex characteristics. Her parents might have been unsure about her gender. Journalists and comedians much later openly doubted her sex. Speculation that Zofia wanted to change her gender started in 1935. By the end of 1936 Zofia had secretly visited the gynecology unit in the "Infant Jesus Hospital" (Szpital Kliniczny Dzieciatka Jezus) in Warsaw. There she decided to become Witold. At first, he tried to keep the operations private, but in April 1937 Witold informed the press with a statement on his gender change. Of course this attracted a lot of attention in Poland. After the operation, he told the press, he decided to change his name to Witold Stanislaw Smętek. A month later the sex change was completed in the aforementioned hospital. Witold told the Australian press: "I had made up my mind to undergo an operation to change sex. I long ago became a great enthusiast for football [soccer], and later on went in for other strenuous sports, and finally I became the champion javelin-thrower of Poland."

After the operations Witold was summoned before a sports commission in Lodz, but at the same time received a call for the Polish army. In 1939 Witold gave an interview to Reuters stating that he wanted to change his sex again back to female. The previous three years had been an ordeal for him. This was the year that Witold lived in France. In France the writer Marcel Allain published the biography *Confession amoureuse de la femme qui devint homme* (Amorous confessions of the woman that became a man). The word "amoureuze" in the title of this biography is somewhat confusing. Allain was the author of cheap detective novels and that explains a lot. We don't know if the second series of operations—back to female—were ever performed.

The war broke out in Europe, and everybody forgot about the woman that became a man. It was often assumed that Witold had died during the war but later, Witold completed university studies in Polish history in 1955. After this, Witold became a tourist guide in Warsaw. He worked for the PTTK, a non-governmental Polish tourist agency. He died in 1983 in Warsaw.

The story of Witold Smetęk is one of the preliminaries that led to the first gender verifications in 1936 at the Berlin Olympics.[1]

Three "male hermaphrodites" were banned from competition at the 1936 Olympics.[2] The athletes involved were never publicly named. However, we do know that gender verification was performed during the Berlin Games. The American sprinter and double gold medalist Helen Stephens was tested after being accused of being a male fraud by the Polish and American press.[3] The *Daily Mail* even wrote, "She is not one of the exquisite beauty queens." Different times, different mores. Stephens was cleared by a German gynecologist. She was not an imposter; she was not intersex. But three others were. In this chapter I want to answer the question of why gender verification started in 1936 and why some women were suspected by the unions, by their fellow competitors and by general public, of being men.

Just before the Summer Olympics in 1936 several athletes underwent gender reassignment. International sports organizations were on alert, prompted by these cases. The media, newspapers and popular magazines in the 1930s reported frequently on the subject of the "man-woman" athlete.

These gender reassignments were the prelude to a far-reaching system of mandatory gender testing that developed after the war.[4]

There are several intersex syndromes, but for this chapter I would like to distinguish between the pre-war transgender athletes that wanted to become men and the post-war athletes that were intersex and wanted to live their lives as they were, as women. Transgender people who wanted to begin living their lives as men were called "man-woman athletes" by the press in 1936. The *Daily Mirror* and the *Daily Express* introduced the "man-woman" to the newspapers in August 1936. The man-woman was defined as a problem for sports organizations. For instance, in May 1936: "Women's sports organizations are taking steps to deal with the man-woman athletes. The subject will be raised jointly by England and Czechoslovakia, each of whom have had a case of a woman athlete being changed by surgical operation into a man."

The man-woman athletes in question were the British shotput athlete Mary Weston and the Czechoslovakian sprinter Zdena Koubkova. Both of them underwent gender reassignment surgery in London in 1936, just before the Olympics. In Germany, physicians also "restored the true sex" or "fixed nature's mistake," as they called their profession. One of their clients was the Belgian cyclist Willy (Elvira) De Bruyne in 1935. She had always felt that she was actually a man. The German doctors used a combination of hormone therapy and surgical intervention.[5] Before his transition Elvira De Bruyne had won the "World Championships" in Antwerp, a race for male cyclists. In this case, women racers were not prohibited. So De Bruyne participated under a male nickname. After his cycling career, he opened—as all the clichés demand—a pub called Café Denderleeuw in Brussels, near the Gare du Nord.

The Women's Amateur Athletic Federation was on its guard. They also had—as they said themselves—to prepare for the "doubtful cases" at the Berlin Olympics in the summer of 1936. These doubtful cases could well be women whose gender was changed through participation in sports. The press introduced a vague (but entirely false) idea of the role of hormones in the physical development of women athletes. In the 1920s and '30s the key role of testosterone in sex development was shown in castrated animals (roosters). Capons would virilize again after being treated with testosterone: that is, their secondary male characteristics returned.

Scientists discovered that although testosterone is the primary male sex hormone, females also produce small amounts of male hormones.

"They say I'm not a girl"

We know now that testosterone plays an important role in both men and women. Testosterone is the fuel for our sex drive. But the hormone also helps the growth and repair of a woman's reproductive tissue, strength and bone mass.

But in the 1930s arose the false idea that the gender of women athletes could change through endogenous "male" hormones. The "fact" that sports could change your body and even your gender through natural hormones was a frequently repeated subject in the (popular) press in the 1930s. The sex of female athletes was controlled by the "balancing act of different hormones and was not absolute," wrote Clare Tebbutt in 2015 in her overview of the articles in the popular press in the 1930s on the man-woman athlete.[6] The human body was, according to the press, a balance between male and female. Gender was therefore not fixed. Sports could change the gender of female athletes. This caused uncertainty about their sex. Gender could change, and sports was the trigger. The general idea was that women that had virilized through sports should be banned from competing with female athletes. Virilization meant that women developed secondary male characteristics, like a deep voice, an Adam's apple, facial hair, and a "lesbian body." Muscularity and homosexuality were regarded as characteristics of masculinization in female athletes. The number of lesbian sportswomen was probably relatively large, but of course not related to sports. Sports was the eminent opportunity to meet other girls in an all-girl activity. It still is, especially when compared to men's soccer.

Modern soccer attracts many LGBT women. In the 2015 World Cup, there were 18 out LGBT athletes playing.[7] The men's game has not welcomed homosexual players yet. The problem is not the soccer field but the locker room. Men's teams tend to be horrified by the idea that a male homosexual player will join them under the showers. This is my personal hypothesis, but there is a dominant culture that starts with the men joking that you shouldn't drop the soap while showering. I don't think competitors would mind a good homosexual player on the team as long as he showered somewhere else. In 2013 there was a disagreement on Dutch television about homosexuality in soccer. The former player René van der Gijp said, "There might be one or two homosexuals, but soccer is no sport for gays. They stop playing at an early age because they'd rather spend their weekends working in a barber shop."

In the 1920s some athletes were openly gay, like Lily Parr and the French Violette Morris. This might have played a role in the decision to take women's soccer from a professional level and return it to amateur status in England. Explaining their decision, the FA released a statement in which it concluded that football was "quite unsuitable for females and ought not to be encouraged."[8] Moreover, several doctors agreed that the sport posed a serious physical risk to women. Not for the last time, a group of men were legislating what women were allowed to do with their bodies.

The IOC had also been reluctant to allow women to participate in the Olympic Games. Prince Franz Josef of Liechtenstein, a member of the International Olympic Committee, spoke for many when he said he wanted to "be spared the aesthetic spectacle of women trying to look and act like men." According to Susan K. Cahn, history professor at the University at Buffalo, participation in sports for women was discouraged. Competing in sports didn't only endanger fertility, it also made women unattractive to men. As a reaction to these blatantly sexist attitudes, women started organizing their own games.[9]

In France, (the now respected) Alice Milliat was a devoted soccer fan. She organized the first international female soccer match between France and England. There's a famous picture of the team captains kissing each other on the mouth before the match. Milliat had to stop her soccer activities, but she did not give up that easily. In 1919 Milliat asked the IAAF to include women's track and field athletics events in the 1924 Olympic Games. The IAAF refused. On October 31, 1921, Milliat formed La Fédération Sportive Féminine Internationale (FSFI) to organize international women's sporting events. The FSFI decided to hold a Women's Olympic Games, which would include all sports, rather than the restricted number open to women in the official Olympics helmed by Pierre de Coubertin.[10] De Coubertin was not amused; he wanted to reserve the word "Olympic" for his organization.

One of the women that participated in the feminine games of Alice Milliat was the French super athlete Violette Morris. Her slogan was "anything a man can do, Violette can do too." Morris's first appearance was at these games; her last appearance was in a Citroën traction event in Normandy. She was killed in an ambush by the French resistance at the end of World War II.

Morris was born in France in 1883. She was a natural athlete, only 5 foot 5 but with a bicep circumference of nearly 14 inches. She excelled at boxing, the javelin throw, shotput, swimming, discus, cycling, soccer and in later years as a motor car racer. In fact, there was no sport she did not play. She played tennis and was selected for the French water polo team.

"They say I'm not a girl"

She was an all-around sports woman and according to the historian Anne Sebba, "She was described as a colossus." Morris was a cross dresser, always in pants and necktie, although wearing pants had been outlawed for women since Napoleon ruled over France. She smoked furiously and was extremely foul mouthed. According to allegations, she used amphetamines and generously shared them with her sports friends. She was quite a character. She fulfilled all the prejudices against sports women.

Violette Morris won two gold medals and one silver medal at the Women's World Games organized by Milliat. But because of her dressing in men's attire and her free lifestyle, she was refused her license renewal by the FSFI. This led to her being banned from the 1928 Olympics in the Netherlands. The official reason was cited as her lack of morals, evidenced by her obvious penchant for wearing men's clothing, her lesbian lifestyle and her violent punching of a soccer referee.

By these measures she was probably pushed into the arms of the Nazis. And pushed into a racing car. She was good, and a well-respected racing car driver. In 1927 she won the Bol d'Or, a 24-hour endurance race in France, at the wheel of a B.N.C. To fit behind the wheel she underwent elective mastectomy: Her large breasts were amputated at her own request. But even in car racing she was once again disqualified for wearing men's clothing, although it's hard to imagine a woman in a dress behind the wheel of a half-open car. You can, by the way, still find lots of photographs of Violette on the web in her racing car, always smoking a cigarette.

Her life had always been connected to sports, and this life was now completely taken away from her. Filled with frustration, she opened a Paris store selling racing car parts, even building racing cars with her employees. I don't think anybody in France liked her as a sportswoman or as a human being. The Nazi Sicherheitsdienst recruited her at her all-time low. She was easy prey. She spied for the Nazis for several years before the war, giving away detailed information about the Maginot Line. Collaborating with the enemy was in deep contrast to her driving an ambulance during the First World War. She served thus at the battles of Verdun and at the Somme. Anne Sebba writes: "It was really driving over rough and dangerous terrain, past the trenches—collecting stretchers of bloody soldiers. It was absolutely critical to get these seriously wounded French soldiers to hospital fast. This is where she discovered that she was really extremely strong and extremely fearless." After the war she dumped her husband and started, or rather continued, wearing trousers, as she had done when driving an ambulance.

She found more acceptance in 1930s Germany, where she lived for a while. As a reward for her services, the former athlete was invited to watch the Berlin Games from a seat in Hitler's box in the Olympic Stadium. She was finally going to the Olympics, but disappointingly as a spectator. In the meantime, she lived in Paris on a houseboat on the River Seine. During the war her task was to foil the British organizations that supported the French resistance. She became an extremely sadistic Nazi, nicknamed the "French Hyena." Morris tortured women with a whip to extract information. The victims often regained consciousness lying naked on the couch of Violette Morris. Some historians, however, think that the torture was played up by the French resistance to justify the accidental killing of two children that were in the car she was driving as she was executed. Morris was sentenced to death in absentia and was killed on a small country road in Normandy in 1944 in an attack that also took the lives of a family with the two children. No one claimed Violette's bullet-riddled body and she was eventually buried in a mass grave in Normandy.[11]

Violette Morris cannot be called an ambassador for sportswomen in France or even the rest of Europe. She lived up to all the prejudices against sportswomen, but still she was a gender victim. Thus the story of Violette Morris belongs in the preliminaries of this book. Her problematic example created difficulties for other sportswomen. How could they hope to change the image people had of sportswomen when such a strong and controversial woman appeared in the pages of every newspaper? Sportswomen were either men, lesbians, butch, transgender, infertile or man-woman.

There is a hilarious modern documentary on the Norwegian soccer team, in which the Norwegian women's national squad admit: "We suck at football." The beautiful Catherine Dekkerhus has to escape the team because all the team members fall in love with her.[12] The rest of the team consists of lesbian soccer players and she is the only one who can explain the off-side rule. This is a running gag in Europe: women cannot explain the off-side rule in soccer. Times haven't really changed at all; there is still a lot of prejudice against women in sports, although the fans do seem to accept female homosexuality better than male homosexuality in sports. There remains a lot of anger in the crowds directed against gay men on the soccer field.[13]

In the 1920s and later, the track attracted the strong and tall girls, the ugly ducklings, the ones who could finally do what they were good at: play sports. Sports did not turn them into swans, but they enjoyed their play and finally got the appreciation they longed for, like everybody else. The story of the Dutch sprinter Foekje Dillema is the best illustration of this. On the track she was a totally different person than she was in other aspects of her life, finally having fun, finally having friends, finally being good at something and being rewarded for it. This joyful life was stolen from her by the IAAF in July 1950. She went back to her village and did not leave her house for over a year.

Dillema must have been hyperandrogenic; she probably had a high level of testosterone in her blood. Today Caster Semenya is the most well-known female runner with a high T (high testosterone level). This, however, is not a result of her sporting activities. It's her body's own (endogenous) testosterone. Sports stimulates testosterone production but only to a certain level. The more you run the more testosterone breaks down; only weightlifting increases your T-level, but there's a limit to that as well. You won't grow into an elite long- and middle-distance runner through weightlifting; nor will you virilize through running. If that were the case, far fewer women would run. But you can virilize with high doses of synthetic testosterone. Ask Andreas Krieger.

The best known modern "case" is the German shotput athlete Heidi Krieger. Many gender specialists and sports historians know the Heidi Krieger case from the 1980s. In East Germany Krieger was led to believe that innocent injections could enhance her performance. It worked. Krieger became strong and more and more addicted to sporting successes and the accompanying applause. Krieger consented to higher doses of the injections, not knowing it was synthetic testosterone. Very high doses. What she did not know was that the injections didn't just make her stronger, the synthetic hormones changed her gender identity. Scientists have confirmed that very high doses of male synthetic hormones taken during puberty can indeed change the way you feel about your gender. Heidi was more and more convinced that she should reassign her gender.

She became Andreas Krieger after hormone replacement treatment and surgery. It was not until the fall of the Berlin wall that she realized that doping had changed her body and her life completely. She had been systematically but unknowingly doped with male hormones. The treatment was so intense that she wanted to become a man. But even before her sports career she "always had felt out of place and had vague ideas about becoming a boy." The sex reassignment was, however, not her own decision. The East German doping program had made the decision for her.[14]

Does this case mean that the 1930s press was right in their assumption that hormones could change your gender identity? No, because first the natural level of testosterone in women cannot be compared to the high doses of the synthetic testosterone from the East German doping agency. And second: synthetic testosterone has another quality than natural testosterone. They are two different chemicals and work differently.

The pre-war "man-woman" athletes wanted to reassign their gender. The post-war intersex athletes have retained their female gender identity. They live their lives as females, socially and personally. They regard themselves as female, without a doubt. Their core gender identity is female. A high T does not make them want to change their gender. The athletes have a deep sense of being female and would never consider a gender change. This book is mainly focused on these post-war intersex women. The way the public judged the pre-war man-woman athletes had a significant influence on how sports organizations wanted to "deal" with the intersex athletes after the war. Even the way the general public judged female athletes before the war plays a role in the wish (the IAAF would call it the need) for gender verification. Lots of people doubted the gender of some female athletes, sometimes all female athletes. They were called upon to defend themselves against the constant prejudices against female athletes, allegations of being too aggressive (competitive), too muscular, mannish and lesbian. Women had nothing to lose on the track except their fertility and their gender.

Pre-war, post-war … what has World War II to do with the gender question on the tracks? The easy answer is: nothing. Although American women showed that they were perfectly capable of doing men's jobs while the men were off fighting the war, nobody looked upon these working women as men. After the war they returned to their housework and children. Gender roles were still clearly defined. Post-war there have been some man-woman athletes, but not as many as between the two world wars. In the interwar years several athletes underwent gender reassignment. The question is therefore: why are there no intersex athletes in pre-war female competition?

My guess is that there actually were several female intersex athletes. We just don't know their names because they were not barred from competition. Nobody knew they were there. There was no chromosome test, no ultrasound to detect internal testicles and no reliable method of measuring hormone levels in the blood. Some intersex conditions were known as hermaphroditism and each case stood on its own. Scientists distinguished true and pseudo hermaphroditism, with true meaning that a person had both a testicle and an ovary; and pseudo meaning a person with primary characteristics of one sex and secondary sex characteristics of the opposite sex, e.g., a person with testes and a vagina. Real knowledge on intersex didn't start until the 1950s. So until then there wasn't much known about the great variety of intersex conditions. So yes, the intersex athletes that must have been on the tracks were never suspended, because they were not suspected. (Or maybe it would be right to say that all the women athletes were suspects simply for having "mannish" characteristics.)

Intersex athletes remained anonymous although we can assume they were active in competitions. From modern statistics we know that there must have been several female intersex athletes since one in about 425 female athletes is intersex.[15] We know this from the statistics on the number of intersex athletes banned by the IOC between 1972 and 1996. But in pre-war competition they remain unknown, although they likely suffered from medical problems like infertility or absent menstruation. There were only physical, gynecological examinations coupled with rudimentary knowledge. Gynecologists even today have little knowledge on intersex girls. Most doctors have never seen them in their practice,[16] because the syndrome is rare in the general population but not among female athletes. They are good at sports, so they are attracted to the field. They want to do what they are good at, like everybody else.

The first patients with an intersex condition were case studies in the 19th century. Physicians had all sorts of opinions about them, mostly psychological. There was a huge interest in the sexual orientation of the hermaphrodite. The gender was determined by the sexual orientation of the patient. No attempt was made to understand these people, let alone do any systematic research. The first serious research was done in 1942 by Harry Klinefelter. He described a group of men with the same combination of rare physical symptoms: breast growth, small genitals and infertility. The cause was unknown until 1959 when scientists reported that a Klinefelter patient had an extra X chromosome: XXY.

As I will demonstrate in the next chapter, to many scientists, from this point onwards the gender was decided by the chromosomes. In the final analyses the chromosomes dictated the sex of a person. It was in the genes, but in my opinion that is an incomplete view. There's a lot more to one's gender than the genes, of course. From the 1960s onward, chromosome analysis was the new trend in bio-scientific gender studies. So the major sports organizations started using simple chromosome analysis to reach a verdict on the gender of an athlete. Before that time sports organizations relied on examination by a gynecologist.

In earlier days the gynecologist saw the phenotype—not the genes, not the genotype. That is, they saw a girl, a girl with problems like amenorrhea, but knowledge about the cause was absent. In those days most girls with menstruation problems never spoke about it, not even at home with their mothers or sisters. They couldn't. The subject was taboo. So they never visited a specialist and were forced to cope with their problems alone. Most of the girls that were banned in recent years come from rural parts of the world, where it seems they still dare not speak about their big secret even at home.[17] In more urban or developed places, most modern 21st century girls visit a specialist when they have medical problems.

Intersex women before the war were rarely suspended. That all changed after the war, when there was a huge leap in knowledge on sex development and the role of chromosomes. The presence of a Y-chromosome meant the end of your career in female competition. All these medical opinions by sports organizations are dubious, as I will later demonstrate in this book.

For now we do not know the names of other intersex athletes, people who move in between the poles of man and woman, whose biology doesn't fit in one of these two categories. We do know for sure they were there before the war and that they were good at certain sports, especially running and throwing a hammer and discus.

Still there was a lot of suspicion and gossip on the tracks on men, "part-men" and so-called "hermaphrodites." Some women had men's legs, like the late and great Fanny Blankers-Koen, the best female athlete in the last century according to the IAAF. They called her the "queen with men's legs."[18] Then there were the women in transit, becoming male through sports. An easy comparison can be made between the pre-war gossip and slander and the modern suspicion of doping. Almost every successful sportswoman was a suspect.

The German athlete Käthe Krauss was one of these athletes. All the competitors doubted her sex. Even her teammates! Although looks don't matter, in photographs it is easy to see why the competition had their doubts about Krauss. She was tall, strong and flat-chested. Krauss weighed 74 kilos and was 1.76 meters tall (more than 6 feet), which was very tall for 1936 and is still today. She won several medals in the Women's World Games. Krauss was in the German relay track team during the Berlin Games. In the heats the team set a new world record. The team however was disqualified for losing the baton in the finals. Hitler sat in his box and was visibly disappointed by the German team.[19] He hit his fist on his thigh in frustration. He did not present the medals for the relay winners, but instead consoled the German relay team in his box in the Olympic Stadium.

Krauss came in third on the 100-meter sprint. On the platform she gave the Nazi salute, while the winner, Helen Stephens, made a military salute. The silver medal went to the intersex sprinter Stella Walsh. Marie Dollinger, who finished fourth on sprint, had suspicions about her teammate Krauss and later quipped, "I was the only woman in that race!"[20] All the medalists were suspected of being intersex: Helen Stephens, Stella Walsh and Käthe Krauss.

The gossip still goes on in this century, although it centers mainly on doping suspects. Still, there have always been some rumors floating around about female athletes being men or "hermaphrodites." Lots of Romanians, for instance, are that sure that the 1,500-, 3,000- and 5,000-meter medalist Gabriela Szabó is intersex. On top of it her husband/trainer was caught driving with performance enhancing drugs. Szabó was a very successful Olympic champion in Sydney and Atlanta. Her record on the 3,000-meter still stands today. Maybe the gossip is reinforced by the fact that she is Romanian from Hungarian descent. Szabó married her coach and was minister of sport for the Romanian youth. And the fact that her husband told the newspapers recently that she cannot have children stirred up the fire again.[21]

When we cross the Oder, the border of Germany and Poland, we meet a lot of muscular sportswomen such as the sprinter Maria Itkina from Belarus, who was a very muscular woman. She finished three times in fourth place in the Olympics before 1968. She competed in the European Championships, so she had to bring a gender certificate. During the Cold War Russian athletes disappeared off the international stage when the gender test was introduced. The Soviet Russians were not to be trusted. They may have cheated, as the Russians still do on doping. Maria Itkina is one of the Soviet Russian women that were under suspicion of doping or gender fraud. Jarmila Kratochvilova of Czechoslovakia in 1963 set the longest standing world record in women's athletics: 1:53.28 on the 800 meters. Her atypical muscular physique spawned rumors of her gender and of illegal drug use. This was just like the sisters Irina and Tamara Press. The only Soviet Russian athlete that was barred was the sprinter Ewa Klobukowska, but she was tested outside of the Soviet Union, in West Germany. We don't know if the Soviets committed gender fraud, but statistically there must have been more intersex athletes in the Soviet Union than the one documented case of Klobukowska. Of course, several females in the competition had been "criminalized" before they were tested. Doping, on the other hand, was already being used in those years in the Soviet Union. But also, American weightlifters were injected with synthetic testosterone in 1954. Their coach and physician, John B. Ziegler, had developed Dianabol, just after Russian coaches had informed him of positive results on testosterone doping in sports.[22] So maybe the muscular Soviet women were not intersex but on synthetic testosterone. It is sometimes hard to believe that these Soviet ladies ran natural. However, there's no proof. But the fact of doping makes it difficult to suggest that Eastern Bloc athletes were intersex.

The winner of the sprint in 1936, the American Helen Stephens, was tested. We know Walsh was intersex. Krauss was never tested, just like the Press sisters in 1966. Krauss lived all her life as a woman, as did the Press sisters. After their sports careers were over, Irina and Tamar Press were tough ladies in the Soviet army, heroes in Russia. Western countries were sure that they were gender frauds. It was hard to prove, since everything was dim and shady in Communist countries. There's no proof, but would they have wanted to live their whole lives as females while secretly being men? To me that seems doubtful.

So how do we judge the strong and muscular females on the track today? The IOC stated in 2010: "That athletes who identify themselves as female but have medical disorders that give them masculine characteristics, should have their disorders treated."[23] The "characteristics" and the "disorders" were not specified. The message later was: if your testosterone level is in the "male range," have yourself treated, unless you are insensitive to the male hormone. No valid argument was given for this rule.

People still have negative judgments about women with male characteristics. A Belgian newspaper called Caster Semenya "a testosterone bomb," and a Dutch newspaper called her "a genetic freak."[24] Eight-hundred-meter runner Lynsey Sharp totally ignored Semenya after her gold rush in Rio. *The Telegraph* commented, "Semenya will top the podium—yet she can never win."[25] It was true the day these words were published. But times are changing. Semenya gets more and more support from the crowds that first booed her. She deserves the approbation because she always followed the rules and regulations, although this must have been mentally very hard for her.

In this chapter, however, I will discuss athletes that underwent gender reassignment. The man-woman athletes. The athletes that actually wanted to live their lives as men. I discuss these cases because their gender changes were the reason for implementing gender verification in female competition. So who were those transgender athletes—or biological intersex males—in pre-war competition? Nine athletes have been discussed in literature, nearly half of the twenty cases of gender reassignment in the 1930s. Some of them were born with ambiguous genitalia, like Mary Weston. We don't really know the precise gender facts on the other eight, but they were raised as girls. They were not frauds. They had no intention to play unfairly.

Raising children who were born with ambiguous genitalia as girls was the common pre-war procedure. Nowadays these children are carefully screened and in the West the decision on the gender is postponed until the child can make their own decision. But in the first half of the last century you just couldn't do anything about it. The advice was to keep quiet about the matter. "Let it be," said the doctor to the parents of Dora Ratjen. "Da kann man nichts machen" (you cannot do anything about it).

Raising these children as girls was not easy, of course. Moreover, as we shall see in the cases of Austrian skier Erika Schinegger, German high jumper Dora Ratjen and author David Peter Reimer, forcing a gender role on a child can cause great hardship and harm, with lifelong effects.

Nowadays the parents of babies with ambiguous genitalia get medical and psychological assistance by a number of specialists. Together with the parents they carefully plan the route to the gender education of the child and suitable surgery if necessary. The child can make the decision when they are ready. They are thus not forced into a gender. And some of them are even quite content with being intersex.

But in the past boys mistakenly raised as girls had lots of trouble, especially during puberty. They grew facial hair, had ejaculations, thought they were lesbians and had to hide from almost everybody they knew. The brave ones among them chose gender reassignment. It is brave because you just cannot hide from the consequences; from now on they would have to live the life of a male. And that is of course the reason why we know about these transgender athletes.

Before the war our knowledge is limited to the athletes that corrected their gender through surgery. The only athlete that was barred was Zdena Koubkova. But no titles were erased. Koubkova may be considered the most important athlete of the intersex area in elite sports, because he was the direct cause for the wish to implement a system of gender verification. The direct cause was an interview with Zdenêk Koubek in *Time* magazine in 1936:

> "A woman? Bah … She is nothing. A man? Hah … He is everything. There is not anything in the world that is not open to him." So said comely, blue-eyed Zdenêk Koubek last week, through an interpreter, as he sat cross-legged on the deck of the *Ile de France*. Because of his curious medical history, he was journeying to Manhattan to appear in a cabaret. Born in Bohemia 23 years ago, the child was pronounced a girl, christened Zdena Koubkova.[26]

Before his gender reassignment, Koubek was a track athlete from Czechoslovakia. He was a slender, androgynous athlete as we can see in photographs from that time. As the female Zdena Koubkova, he won two medals at the 1934 Women's World Games and several national titles in the 800 meters running, long jump and high jump, and set a few world records in running events in 1936. The Women's World Games were an alternative for the Olympic Games. In the Olympics women only competed in five athletic disciplines. In the Women's Games the athletes competed in twelve disciplines.

Zdena won the 800 meters and came in third on the long jump. In 1938 the World Women's Games were cancelled because the IOC decided to allow women to complete in almost all athletic events. But not on the 800 meters, which was deemed too long and strenuous for women. Therefore Koubek had been performing well in a discipline that was seen as unfit for women. The woman Zdena Koubkova held world records on the 80 and 800 meters (2:12.4 White City, London). Nowadays this is a strange combination of sprint and endurance. After his transition, he was determined to set the world record on the 800 as a man. But instead he became a soccer player. The records he held as a female runner have been erased by the IAAF, although Zdenêk himself was convinced that he would keep the records until one day a girl would beat them. We know this from a very frank interview he gave to the magazine *Your Body* in June 1936.[27]

Zdenêk told the magazine he had to hire a lawyer for the official administrative transition from female to male, supported with medical documents. To become a man, the girl Zdena first had to die. A death certificate was issued after Zdenêk declared that his life as a girl was over. He had killed the girl within him. Zdenêk was then reborn at the age of 22 with a brand-new birth certificate: "recording my entrance in the world as a man."

Zdenêk became an elegant broad-shouldered man with a narrow waist. He gave his dresses to his sister, but they did not fit her, because Zdena had also been a broad-shouldered woman: "She had to alter them to suit her requirements," he told *Your Body*. Koubek went back to the job he previously held in a restaurant (the story doesn't tell if his salary was raised, now being a male waiter).

The operation was quite simple and hadn't hurt him at all. "Now I feel myself positively and completely male." With this sensation he immediately stopped training with the girls. He hoped the military would not make an exception for him and looked forward to his time in the army. "I can easily picture myself in military tunic, and exercising in the courtyard of the barracks with my hair close-cropped." He longed to be a man in every possible way, even considering getting married. He finally did. The interviewer considered him more masculine than many other males of his age who were actually born as men and lived their whole lives as men. "His appearance, speech and gestures and attitude towards life are now these of a virile young man. He is proud to be a man."

Directly after this interview the president of the American Olympic Committee, Avery Brundage, made a proposal at the IOC meeting in 1936: "An American proposal was put forward that all women competitors at the Olympic Games should be medically examined in view of the Koubek case."[28] Brundage wanted to tackle the so-called "man-woman problem" in elite sports. The next day he recommended in a piece in *Time* magazine that "all women athletes entered in the Olympics be subjected to a thorough physical examination to make sure that they were really 100% female."[29]

It is interesting to note that Brundage spoke of complete women, 100 percent. Apparently there was a conception of female athletes that were not 100 percent women. These must have been the doubtful cases. He was probably referring to the so-called hermaphrodites, those women with male gender characteristics. At that time there was some early knowledge about people who exhibited both male and female physiological characteristics. From the end of the 19th century they had been labeled hermaphrodites, although the term is misleading. Hermaphroditism is not an aspect of human nature. Snails and flowers are hermaphroditic; they can procreate along the male and female line. Brundage probably had a vague idea of women with a disorder of sex development. Or maybe he even might have had very concrete ideas about women not being 100 percent female. The implication of his words was that athletes not 100 percent female should be banned from competition.

The first athlete barred after a mandatory gender test was the Dutch athlete Foekje Dillema. She was banned for life after she had refused to submit to a gender verification test. The Dutch Union assumed she was a "hermaphrodite." After her death it was confirmed that she was intersex. Dillema had an imbalance in sex chromosomes.[30]

In 1936 hermaphroditism was not only a question of primary sex characteristics. Researchers had shown that hormones were not explicitly male or female. This served as a rich source for journalists who wrote that sex hormones could alter the sexual characteristics of a trained athlete. In other words, an imbalance in these hormones could cause a spontaneous change of gender. And sport could trigger such an imbalance. Sex was changeable, according to popular magazines in the 1930s. And these magazines were highly influential.[31]

So, men in masquerade and hermaphrodites should be excluded from the female competition, according to Brundage, who became chairman of the IOC in 1952. He was supported by the IAAF and even by the Fédération Sportive Féminine International. This women's federation urged the need for testing: "Some of the women in Berlin looked more like men and the fact that there already have been cases of woman athletes being changed into men by operations is held to make such a discussion very necessary."[32]

There was no solidarity among women athletes. In fact, the Féderation Fémine was fed up with all the man-woman athletes on the tracks and on the soccer fields. Initially the women's liberation movement had financially and morally supported female soccer. The movement eventually turned away from transgenders and the man-woman athlete.

In the twenty known cases of gender reassignment in the 1930s ten patients were former athletes. The first and foremost athletes were the aforementioned Zdeněk Koubek and the shotput athlete Mark Weston. Zdeněk Koubek went on a tour in the United States to star in a cabaret sketch that played on his days as a woman athlete. In the sketch he presented a correlation between masculinity and the female athlete. The audience might have understood that masculinity is a male sex characteristic. Not a female one. Of course we know that muscles can be trained. This does not make a man out of an athlete. The human sex is congenital; there is no natural cause that can change one's sex (apart from women with very rare syndromes).

Koubek got a lot of attention in the American press and talked about his gender reassignment surgery. About his doubts on being female, about people staring at him all the time, about wearing skirts although trousers suited him better, about his operation and the moment he came out of his anesthesia, crying for joy to see his girlfriend at his bedside. He was offered a job in America, but Zdeněk wanted to return to his native country to marry his girlfriend from Slovenia. After the war he took up rugby in the team of his brother Jaroslav in a local club. Koubek lived a quiet life with his wife in Prague and died at the age of 73.

In 1936 Mary Edith Louise Weston became Mark Weston in the Charing Cross Hospital in London. As Mary, Mark was called the Devonshire Wonder. Mary was a British champion in javelin and discus throwing. She wasn't well known on the track but became famous off the field. The sex change gained a lot of attention in the British press: "Woman turns into man. Miss Mary is now Mr. Mark." Sex change had become a modern technical possibility.

The South African–born London surgeon Lennox Broster, who treated Weston, said, "Mark Weston, who has always been brought up as a female, is male and should continue to live as such." He told the press that "Miss Weston looks manly with a well-formed muscular body." Broster even speculated that Weston was a grownup tomboy who "instinctively preferred the company of boys to that of girls. He wanted to wear men's clothes and play men's games such as football."[33] So apart from a masculine body Weston apparently had a male outlook. She transgressed the boundaries between men and women through sports.

According to researchers, this was the first successful gender reassignment in history. Mark married his childhood girlfriend Alberta Bray in August 1936. Alberta had helped Mark in his transition. She was in fact the main reason for him wanting surgery. The couple had three children. For this Mark had to be biologically male from the start. He was born with testicles.

We might even assume that the surgeon was easily convinced to perform the operation, not even because of the primary sex characteristics but because of the secondary characteristics. Competing in sports was seen as unnatural for women, causing those who were highly motivated to play sports to be regarded as aggressive and mannish, and a muscular body was seen as a secondary male characteristic. Muscular women were also suspicious to their opponents and seen as male frauds. In most cases these women were considered to be completely male. The notion of their being males was reinforced by the many cases of gender reassignment before the war. Lots of people might have assumed that sports made men out of females—that sport brought changes to the sex and gender of female athletes, and if they weren't already male, sports made them male. Females left their gender on the track. Sports gave them male bodily features, like muscularity. Becoming stronger might even motivate the girls to reassign their gender, was a general opinion between the wars. Medical organizations that advised the government in Great Britain had a strong opinion about discouraging sports for women. Some forms of sports could even be dangerous for girls, they maintained.

After the operations Mark returned his medals, because he "didn't deserve them." But in the statistics of the Women's World Games the victories and records of Koubek and Weston were not erased. You could probably say that Weston still earned his titles and medals, because officially he was a she on the track. The public did not understand this either. If he was a she then she had a right to the titles. After all, she was a girl athlete in those days. It was pretty confusing for the readers of the newspaper articles. If she had changed her gender by a series of operations she once must have been a woman.

With two athletes that underwent a gender reassignment and more to come, sex change was to become kind of a trend in women's athletics, such that the general public made a connection between athletics and the desire to become a man. Female athletes probably all had a desire to be a man, became the general opinion on women in sports. This was especially held to be true for the women in disciplines like the javelin throw and shotput which were seen as requiring manly qualities. It came as no surprise for the people who believed these disciplines were inappropriate for women.

Was there a direct correlation between disciplines such as shotput, javelin and discus throw, the 800-meters run and the desire to become a man? One could think so by the number of cases presented in this chapter. But this is far from the truth, of course.

So why were there several transgender people in these disciplines? I hazard to guess that the athletes were in fact biological males at birth but were not recognized as such by their parents or doctors. They later must have felt that they were men instead of women. The fact that four women athletes fathered children after their reassignment provides strong evidence. You cannot make testicles out of ovaries, although the general public in those days before the war might have believed so.

Both Koubek and Weston wanted gender reassignment desperately. One of their motives was to legally marry their beloved girlfriends. We do not know the motivation of the other athletes discussed in this chapter. But the link between female athletes and wanting to become a man was easily made in the press and by the public. This confirmed all the prejudices on female athletes being actually males or wanting to be males. There was a direct relation—although the press did not spell it out—between female sport and being male or wanting to be or even becoming male through sports or surgery. And the possibility of changing gender through surgery was new for mankind.

The New Zealander Peter Alexander—formerly known as Mavis Huggins—recounted in a Pathé newsreel, with a pipe in his hand and a woman by his side: "I was born and educated as a girl, but men's sports have always appealed to me particularly. I'm very fond of golf, very keen on swimming and tennis. I decided to give it up as I felt I had a decided advantage over my opponents."[34] From this statement we might assume he knew something was different with his sex development. Why give up if you're a winner? It doesn't make sense.

But it always would have been impossible for real fraud, a man in masquerade on the track. It's quite impossible to live half your life as a boy and then compete as a woman. There will always be people who knew you were a boy before you went into competition. Men in masquerade do not exist in sports. No man was ever caught during the days sex testing became compulsory. The biological men in competition were raised as girls by their parents. Gender fraud is not an aspect of sports that can be taken seriously.

Most of the athletes that underwent gender reassignment came from Central Europe. There's no explanation for this other than maybe the willingness and skill of performing the surgery in these countries. The athletes came from Germany, Poland, Czechoslovakia and two from England. Apart from the two most well-known cases there were others, like Zofia Smetkovna, Stepanka Pekarova, Ida Ehrl, Erika Matthes and Edith Hallstead. Why so many? Obviously, they were good at sports and were attracted to the field. Like everybody else they did what they were good at. And they were physically equipped for the game. They were generally taller and stronger than their competitors. They could be expected to be good at many sports.

The same goes for the British javelin specialist Edith Halstead, who became Eddie Halstead. In 1933 Edith won the International University Games and got a silver medal in the British Empire Games of 1934. Edith was born into an athletic family; her sister Nellie was a talented runner.

Ida Ehrl was also a talented runner. In the European Championships—the first championships for women—she came in fourth, after the intersex sprinter Stella Walsh, Käthe Krauss (who was under suspicion) and the late and great Dutchwoman Fanny Blankers-Koen. Blankers-Koen was a mother of two when she won four gold medals at the 1948 Olympics in London. She was the best female athlete of the last century, according to the IAAF (Jesse Owens was the best male athlete). We don't know a lot about Ida Ehrl, who came in fourth, but it is said that she also changed her gender.

The Czechoslovakian Stepanka Pekárová was a pentathlon athlete: shotput, high jump, long jump, sprint and hurdles. Her best years were 1934 in the ladies' Olympiad and in 1935 in the University Games. We have little knowledge of her other than the fact that she underwent a gender reassignment and became Stepan Pekar. The pictures we have of her show an athlete with a receding hairline that is common in men. She changed her gender in May 1936. Pekar studied medicine in Prague. There is little knowledge on him in the public domain. All we know is the press comment on the back of her pictures before and after the surgery. The comment states:

> For the second time in two years the Czechoslovakian Athletic Commission had to change officially the status of one of its athletes from woman to man. Recently miss Stepanka Pekárová was declared to be a man by a medical board. She had been examined two years ago and at that time was found to be a woman. In May 1936 Miss Pekárová posed for a picture after a track meet.

We see her as a woman with two simple hairpins. And a second picture shows a man in a man's shirt and trousers.

Just after the war, in 1946, two French women athletes chose gender reassignment after their sports career. Their names, Lea (later Leon) Caurla and Claire (later Pierre) Bressolles, are still on the IAAF list of the 1946

European Athletic Games. They both won the silver medal in the relay. Both athletes fathered children after the gender reassignment. They were the last two track and field athletes who escaped the sex test, because four years later the IAAF introduced gender verification and the first victim was the Dutch intersex sprinter Foekje Dillema.

The XX-Games

A Short History of Gender Verification

The Olympic charter states: "The practice of sport is a human right. Every individual must have the possibility of practicing sport, without discrimination of any kind and in the Olympic spirit, which requires mutual understanding with a spirit of friendship, solidarity and fair play." The catch is in the last two words: "fair play." The IOC defines intersex as unfair play. Thus, intersex athletes had no right to play sports in the elite competition— just like doping sinners and other cheats, who all fall in the same category of unfair play. The main difference is that intersex athletes are not frauds, whereas doping sinners are. After all, intersex athletes have no intention to cheat. They just want to do what they are good at. Like everybody else. Nevertheless, they were barred by the dozens. We know from statistics that on the average one in 400 to 450 female athletes was barred between 1972 and 1996. Some scientists even state that the prevalence of a disorder of sex development is 7 per 1,000 female elite athletes.[1]

The history of gender verification in elite female competition is a sordid one. And there is a long, 80-year history of vigorously trying to unmask gender frauds. In this chapter you will find an overview of eight decades of gender verification in elite sports.

To most people gender verification seems quite simple: "Drop your pants and I tell you what you are. Penis is male, vagina is female." But in rare cases it's not that easy. What would they say if presented with a person with a vagina and internal testes? Chances are that they would now say: "Then she is a man." From the perspective of the geneticist we would say: "This person has sex chromosomes XY, she's a male." The endocrinologist would say: "She's female, because male hormones are useless for her." The psychologist would say: "She regards herself as female, so she is female." The city's registry office would say: "The birth certificate states 'female.' She is an assigned woman." The competition would say: "Just look at her! She's a man." And if she just dropped her pants everybody would say: "She's female."

So there you have it in a nutshell. It is a complex question. There are many answers to the question whether this person is male or female. Scientists have tried to define male and female but they fail to give a definition, because every definition fails.

The best answer yet would be to say that the person is intersex, in between man and woman. But I do feel that we should respect the answer she would give herself: "I'm female. I was born and raised as a girl. I live my life as a female. Do not call me male!" In this chapter I'm looking at her as an athlete and the way she is treated by the competition and sports organizations. But always with respect to her own opinion.

The first intersex athletes were suspended from the Olympics in 1936.[2] A Dutch medical publication mentions the disqualification of three "male pseudo hermaphrodites." The term male pseudo hermaphrodite is a person with testes and a female appearance. In less enlightened times doctors called intersex people hermaphrodites. The correct term is, however, intersex; the syndrome is called Disorder of Sex Development (DSD).

At least two other athletes would have never stood the test on that Olympiad of 1936. The first one was Dora Ratjen, the German high jumper who turned out to be a biological man, although he was not a fraud. He was raised a girl. The second athlete was the Polish-American sprinter Stella Walsh. After her brutal death in 1982 the coroner concluded she had a male Y-chromosome, but more X than Y. Due to an imbalance in X and Y she was intersex, and would have been sent away in 1936 if she had been "suspect" at the Berlin Games. Her direct competitor Helen Stephens, a strapping, six-foot-tall American farm girl, was summoned to visit a German gynecologist, and was cleared.[3] You will of course find their life stories in this book.

Before the Second World War there were, as we have seen, several female athletes that underwent gender reassignment. That is why the chairman of the United States Olympic Committee, Avery Brundage, proposed to the other members of the IOC to establish gender verification for all the athletes in the next Olympiad. Brundage made this proposal directly after the publication of an interview in *Time* magazine with the Czech track and field athlete Zdenek Koubek. Like other laymen, Brundage thought that women could virilize through sports—that is, develop male secondary sex characteristics—and worse, could even become biological men. So

Brundage, later the fifth chairman of the IOC, thought it was high time for gender verification.[4, 5]

Avery Brundage was at that time chairman of the United States Olympic Committee (USOC), president of the United States Athletic Union and vice president of the IAAF. He was in the driver's seat of sports. Brundage was, like so many other managers in sports, a very authoritarian man with influence in all aspects of sports.[6] He was in charge.

Brundage proposed a mandatory gender verification starting at the 1940 summer games in Tokyo. His proposal was discussed at the IOC session in Berlin 1936 where Tokyo was selected as host for the 1940 games. The discussion between IOC members was deep and complex, because determining who is eligible for the female Olympic Games and who is not is complex. The opposition against a system of mandatory gender testing was too strong inside the IOC at that time. The proposal was therefore abandoned.

There wouldn't, however, be any Olympic Games for the next 12 years due to the Second World War. Japan was in 1940 already at war with the Soviet Union. Hitler proposed that the 1940 games could again take place in Berlin. But he had other plans than just sports. "Sports is," as George Orwell wrote, "war without the shooting," and Hitler preferred the shooting. He attacked Poland in 1939. England and France declared war on Germany and the second great war had begun.

The games of 1948 in London were the first games after Berlin and after the war. But there was no mandatory gender verification in London, aside perhaps from suspect cases. The IOC began mandatory testing at the height of the Cold War, in 1968.

The International Amateur Athletic Federation (IAAF), however, started a mandatory verification for the European Championships in Brussels in August 1950.[7] Brundage as vice-president of the IAAF must have had a decisive influence on the decision to start compulsory testing at official championships.[8]

It's not surprising that through the years so many track and field athletes were suspended. The IAAF was the first and the last organization preoccupied with the search for men in masquerade and hermaphrodites (as they were labeled in the 1950s). I cannot think of any other reason why so many track and field athletes were barred. It must have been the endeavor of the IAAF presidents. In 2018 Sebastian Coe, chairman of the IAAF, proposed new rules on the classification of females,[9] after so many other forms of regulations through the years had failed one after the other; and after so much humiliation. The IAAF seems obsessed with gender fraud.

In August 1950 all athletes in the female competition had to bring a so-called certificate of femininity to Brussels. The verification was done by gynecologists in the athlete's native country. The IAAF continued mandatory gender verification until 1992. That year the organization admitted that there had been no gender frauds in the history of testing in athletics.[10]

In 1992 the IAAF started doping control and the inspector would be able to see via a urine test if an athlete was a gender fraud. But the IAAF also kept an eye on "suspect cases." And indeed they suspended several intersex women after 1992.[11]

The first verifications in the 1950s and '60s were physical examinations by a gynecologist. In 1950 the Dutch 200-meter specialist Foekje Dillema refused to go to the mandatory "medical examination." She must have known she wouldn't pass this test.[12]

The intersex athletes were all assigned female at birth and raised as girls. In lots of cases they didn't know themselves that they had a disorder of sex development (DSD). Some women live their entire lives without knowing this. Elite intersex athletes heard the astonishing verdict after a genealogical examination. A gynecologist in 1950 would use a number of routines and scales to form a judgment on a possible disorder of sex development of the athlete: body hair patterns, menstruation, anatomy and of course examination of the genitals.

Before an explanation of the examination, it's best to hear the voice of one of the victims. Mary Peters, gold medalist in Munich 1972 in pentathlon, is quoted as having described her experience with the gynecological examination as "the most crude and degrading experience I have ever known. I was ordered to lie on the couch and pull my knees up. The doctors proceeded to undertake an examination which, in modern parlance, amounted to a grope. Presumably they were looking for hidden testes. They found none and I left."[13] Peters felt abused. She probably was.

Still, the gender verification was more than groping young athletes. Unusual body hair patterns can give clues to certain syndromes, mostly caused by male hormones. It can range from no body hair at all to excessive male hair patterns on the face and the body. The role of hormones was known in 1950, although testosterone levels couldn't be measured in the blood. Males and females have different hormone levels and different hair patterns on their body and face. Excessive levels of male hormones in women (hyperandrogenic) can cause a divergent hair pattern on the female body. These patterns can be caused by syndromes of the adrenals, the ovaries or by internal testes. Although these testes are small and infertile, they still produce elevated levels of testosterone. Intersex women that are sensitive to these high levels of testosterone tend to have male patterns of body hair. Facial hair, for instance. But there are also intersex woman who are completely insensitive to testosterone. These women have no body hair, not even pubic hair. As of 1961 physicians used the Ferriman-Gallwey Scoring Card for hirsutism (excessive body hair). The scoring card, which can easily be found on the Internet, was a simple black and white card with female images and different body hair patterns on their body and face. The scoring card was widely used in the practice of medicine. It is important to note that half of the women with mild patterns of male body hair have normal testosterone levels.[14]

The second aspect of the gynecological examination would be a review of the menstruation cycle. Playing sports on a high level can cause amenorrhea, absence of menstruation. Women and girls who play sports sometimes skip one or more periods. A total absence of menstruation—never having had any period at any age—for a senior athlete is cause for concern. There can be a number of syndromes causing this. The most severe would be an intersex condition; a woman without ovaries will never menstruate. Total absence of menstruation would not be a decisive factor for a diagnosis of intersexuality, but it adds up to other medical factors.

Inspection of the genitals is the third examination procedure used by the gynecologist. Internal testes are, for instance, sometimes palpable in the groin. An intersex woman usually lacks a uterus, and the vaginal cavity is shallow. Furthermore, the clitoris can be enlarged by male hormones. Other anatomy is also a factor that can add up to a diagnosis, such as body length, hips, breasts size. The gynecologist would form his diagnosis on these physical characteristics. The athlete in the 1950s would not be informed of the diagnosis by the gynecologist.[15] The diagnosis would be communicated to the local athletic union. The athlete was then informed by her national union. Other athletes would get a signed certificate. The Dutch speed skater Yvonne van Gennip told me the enclosed letter stated: "Congratulations, you're a woman."[16] That was 1988 in Canada.

The first certificates of femininity were brought from the athlete's native country to the championships. This meant the athlete visited a hospital in her own country, acting upon instructions by the national federation.

"They say I'm not a girl"

The athletes received a letter that stated they were expected on a certain day for a medical test. The Dutch girls, for instance, had to go to a hospital in the Hague on Saturday, July 8, 1950.[17] The English sprinter Sylvia Cheeseman told me that she went to the championships forgetting all about the test and was therefore summoned to visit the academic hospital in Brussels to get her examination.[18] She did. She got her certificate.

In 1954 the countries of the Soviet Union rejoined the European Athletic Championships after more than 30 years. The athletes had already participated in the games of Helsinki in 1952, but without sex testing. The Soviets astonished the world with their female athletes and they defeated the American females on the medal count. A total number of 23 Soviet ladies went home with an Olympic title, against just nine American women. Four years later the Soviets were the strongest contenders in the world, male and female.

But in 1954 the Soviet Union was for the first time confronted with the phenomenon of gender verification by the IAAF. In the 1960s Tamara and Irina Press dominated on a variety of track and field events: shotput, javelin, hurdles, pentathlon and relay. The Presses were two Jewish sisters from the Ukraine, whose father had been killed on the front in the Second World War. Their mother took the girls to Samarkand where they joined an athletic club. Both Irina and Tamara were talented. Tamara won four Olympic medals; Irina won two gold medals. Due to Tamara's masculine appearance critics were convinced that they were both male, and called them disdainfully "the Press Brothers." Tamara and Irina are still mistrusted. They even had a bad influence on sport for girls in the 1960s. Dick Bank, swimming coach, told the *Los Angeles Times*:

> One thing that held back women's track ... was the image given the sport by such athletes as Tamara Press of the Soviet Union. In some ways ... she obviously had more male characteristics than female. Parents in this country would see pictures of her and decide that if that was the kind of people they had in women's track they would get their daughters to go swimming or something else.

It appeared that Americans and Europeans were, more than the Soviets, obsessed with the notion of who was male or female, or female enough, for the elite competition.

The IOC started mandatory verification at the highest point of the Cold War in 1968 at the winter games, with a rather subjective effect. IOC chairman Avery Brundage remarked in the *Los Angeles Times* in August

1970 that the athletes "had become more feminine now."[19] So finally sports appeared to have reaped the benefits of his 1936 proposal. The Olympic Games were back on their mission to become the most exciting beauty contest in the world.

At this point, the IAAF mistrusted the gender verification done by the Soviet countries. If ever there was any. So the IAAF decided to transfer the testing to the location of the championships. On-site testing so there could be no (more) gender fraud.

Tamara and Irina both ended their careers that year, and so the critics were now sure that the Press sisters were indeed frauds. But were they? Both lived their entire lives as female. And people should not be presumed guilty before their guilt is proven. According to the declaration of human rights they are to be considered innocent. The Press sisters were never tested on location so we have to assume they were both female. Irina died in 2004 but Tamara is still living. I do not believe they were male imposters.

However, it is possible that they could have been both hyperandrogenic—that is, athletes with a high testosterone level. Congenital Adrenal Hyperplasia has after all a very high prevalence in Ashkenazi female Jews.[20] In this syndrome the brain signals to the adrenals to produce stress hormones (cortisol). But due to an enzyme defect the adrenals cannot produce cortisol, but instead react by secreting higher levels of testosterone. More than 30 percent of Ashkenazi Jews are carriers of the genetic mutation. The prevalence of the mutation is four percent. My theory would be that girls with a high T-level might be good at some athletic disciplines and thus pursued what they could do best. A form of natural selection. After all, sport is natural selection; the athlete with the "best" genes wins. But even if the Press sisters were hyperandrogenic they would not have been disqualified at a gender verification in 1968, because they would be "complete" women. The sisters themselves claim that they ended their relatively long careers to take care of their mother.

The first gender verifications by the IAAF on location went into the history books as "nude parades." The IAAF decided to test all athletes at the same time by a panel of three gynecologists from the East and West. The athletes had to line up naked or almost naked and go past this medical panel. It was a very humiliating procedure but at the time there was not much public outcry because, as Kidd Bruce wrote, "They flew under the radar."

The U.S. shotput athlete Maren Seidler stood in the parade at the Pan American Games in Winnipeg in 1967: "They lined us up outside a room where three doctors were sitting in a row behind desks. You had to go in and pull up your shirt and push down your pants. Then they just looked while you waited for them to confer and decide if you were O.K. It really was hideous…. I just felt it was humiliating." A skinny athlete passed her on the way back and told Seidler she was sent away because "she had a flat chest."[21]

Not everyone was disappointed in the results of this procedure. Pat Connolly, a pentathlon competitor, said, "We had to take a very embarrassing sex test. But with the idea of fairness in mind, we complied with the test, happy that at last the men would be eliminated from our competition."[22] Other athletes just made a big joke of it: "It was just plain dumb!"

Connolly was just like many other athletes: afraid that the female competition was in fact a secret mixed competition. The notion of unfair competition is strong among the athletes themselves. On the other hand, every disadvantage has an advantage: If you lose you can always find comfort in the idea that you were beaten by a man and that you were the best female in the field.

A small research study among athletes in Lillehammer showed that about 70 percent of the women found gender verification useful. Twenty percent expressed the view that the test was humiliating.[23] And that was in 1994, when the tests were performed in the lab on cells obtained from the inner cheek.

In 1996 Atlanta 82 percent of the female athletes were in favor of gender testing.[24] An overwhelming majority were afraid of an unfair competition. Remarkable, because by this time it had only become more and more difficult to commit gender fraud. And of course it's sometimes hard to guess whether a person you meet is a man or a women. In social interactions a person's gender is one of the first things we ordinarily determine. You can't just walk up to someone and ask, "Sorry, what is your gender?" That's intrusive and awkward for both parties. So by testing you can be sure any men in the competition are eliminated. But the point is: there never was male fraud in competition. I can understand the uncertainty. But it's practically impossible if you lived your pre-athletic life as a boy to turn up as a girl on the athletics tracks. Probably everyone, friend and foe, would tweet: "She's a man!" And where would he shower? Besides, modern sportswear conceals little. Even in a winter sport like speed skating. How can people say that Caster Semenya is a man after seeing her in her barely-there tights? So it wasn't major news when IAAF concluded in 1992 that in 40 years of gender verification they never caught a male fraud in athletics.[25] But the by-catch were a few dozen intersex athletes.

The parades in 1967 were of course not thorough examinations, only cursory and probably just used as a prevention against the idea of biological males in the female competition. I guess these parades were organized to have a deterrent effect on male imposters from the Soviet Union. After all, no male would join the naked female lineup.

Nude parades were first held at the Pan American Games in Winnipeg and in Budapest. Although the athletes were curious themselves about the competition, they did protest against these humiliating procedures. This had to stop. It stopped of course; athletes could not be treated like cattle. The Polish Ewa Klobukowska stood in the "nude parade" in Budapest, but was later barred on a chromosome count in Germany.

In the late 1950s the first karyotyping was done. A karyotype is a simple graphic of the chromosomes in a cell. Chromosomes can be stained with certain chemicals so a scientist can identify and count the chromosomes. By that time geneticists had discovered that some people have more than 46 chromosomes. Klinefelter men, for instance, have 47 chromosomes (47XXY). They have three sex chromosomes in a cell. This research was published in 1959.[26] But this was far too intensive for testing a couple hundred athletes. A new simple gender verification test was introduced in 1968. The test was called the Barr Body Test. Just a little bit of saliva was enough to count the number of X-chromosomes in the cells of an athlete. It was a simple and cheap test and great numbers of athletes could be tested in just a short time. So in the winter of 1968, the IOC joined in with this new procedure. In the same year the IOC introduced a mandatory gender verification, more than 30 years after Avery Brundage proposed such a procedure in Berlin 1936. The discussion of mandatory gender verification in the IOC had been complex, more profound and the opposition within the IOC was strong. The IAAF and the IOC had been debating for years about each other's standpoints. But the Cold War sped up the decision-making process. The Soviets were suspected of gender fraud and hormone doping in their endeavor to beat the Americans at the Olympic Games. Dr. Nahum Sternberg, a medical advisor to the Soviet Ministry of Sports from 1956 to 1965, told Leo Heiman of Copley News

Services, cited in *The Los Angeles Times* in March 1968, that "the Russians have used hormones to change boys into girls and to make women athletes more masculine."

Yes, you can change the phenotype of a man through surgery, but not his genotype. That is, through hormones and surgery you can make a woman out of a man and vice versa. But the genetic makeup of the cells always remains the same. A trans woman (male to female) still has genotype XY. All her body cells contain a Y chromosome. The idea behind a chromosome test for athletes must have been that you couldn't fool the geneticist. There was and still is the conception that in the end the sex chromosomes define your gender: XX is female, XY is male. Of course, even the biologic gender is more complicated—there are XX-men and XY-females. But in the 1960s the genetic makeup would tell with which sex chromosomes you were born. There could be no cheating. And with a simple lab test you could count and identify the X-chromosomes. The IOC gave in, and the Cold War was the catalyst. Let's do our biology homework again.

Chromosomes are strings of DNA. They come in pairs, thin strands twisted around each other like spiral staircases. The chromosomes can be found in the core of each body cell. Chromosomes can be stained with chemicals, so they become visible through color. Chromo is Greek for color. Each pair is formed by one chromosome from the father and one from the mother. Human beings usually have 46 chromosomes in 23 pairs, with one of those pairs being the sex chromosomes. All chromosomes are numbered except the sex chromosomes. This is not because these chromosomes look like X or Y. Hermann Henking, who discovered the X in 1890, wasn't sure that this material was a chromosome. So for the time being he labeled the object "X." And Y follows X in the alphabet. So when the male chromosome was identified by Nettie Stevens, she labeled it "Y." This proved to be useful in the end. Even in genetics your gender counts.

A gene is a segment of DNA on a chromosome. Genes are made up from DNA. You might say that a gene holds the instruction for certain characteristics. Your gender, for instance, and body height, eye color and a nose in front of your face. There are about 20,000 human genes on 46 chromosomes. Around 150 genes are involved in athletic performance.[27] For example, there is the gene numbered ACTN3, the speed gene. There's a gene on the Y-chromosome that codes for body height. Men tend to be taller than women. Intersex athletes are on the average taller than other female athletes. The cause is a gene on the Y-chromosome.[28] But body height is not considered unfair in sports. Body height, like strength, is one of the main differences between men and women, and both are essential for athletic performance. Height matters! But only strength is considered as essential and unfair.

By 1968 the IOC joined the IAAF in their endeavor to unmask male frauds. From now on an athlete in the female competition needed two X-chromosomes. The "XX-Games" started in the winter of 1968. The winter of our discontent. The Barr Body Test showed that the athlete had two X-chromosomes. What is a Barr Body?

A Barr Body is an inactive X-chromosome in a female body cell. Female cells contain two X-chromosomes, but just one can be active in a cell. Two X's is lethal for a cell. So in every cell with two X-chromosomes, one X is silenced. Just one X is expressed in a cell, at random the X of the mother or the X of the father. The inactivated X is called a Barr Body and can be seen as a dense, dark-staining spot on the edge of an XX-cell. The Barr Body is named after the Canadian scientist Murray Barr, who first described the inactivated X in cells of female cats (a cat has 38 chromosomes).

Intersex woman with XY-chromosomes have no Barr Body, for they have just one (active) X. Intersex women with two types of cells, XX and XY, have a Barr Body in part of their cells. The Barr Body Test was introduced at the Olympic Winter Games in Grenoble, 1968.[29] The athlete was asked to give a bit of salvia from the inner mouth, technically called a buccal smear. This is where body cells are quickly renewed and fresh. The laboratory assistant looked for a Barr Body in a sample of cells from the athlete. Athletes in the female competition without a Barr Body would be asked for further physical examination. It is estimated that 10 percent of this population left without further examination. That's a pity because the Barr Body Test is not reliable, it should be seen as an indication only. The Spanish hurdler Maria Martinez Patiño was—as we shall see—tested twice, once negative, once positive.

With the introduction of the Barr Body Test gender was seen as a result of the chromosomes XX. Years later the IOC would be forced to confirm that sex development is far more complicated than that. But for now the IOC was very enthusiastic about the new, simple lab technique. And the athletes did not need to spread their legs in a gynecologist's chair. The groping was over. But the humiliation of being excluded from the competition remained. From 1968 to 1992 the IOC, the IAAF and probably more sports organizations used the test as a compulsory instrument for female competition. If you were deemed not eligible for a national competition, you would never be selected for an international competition let alone for the Olympic Games. There will therefore never be exact statistics on the number of intersex athletes. I know for instance through my research that in the Netherlands at least four female athletes were barred. But only one case reached the press.[30]

So there are more cases than the IOC or scientists would know about. Geneticist Malcolm Ferguson-Smith concluded that between Munich 1972 and Atlanta 1996, an average of one in 421 athletes were barred from the female competition at the Olympics.[31] Without a doubt more athletes had already been banned by national or international organizations. These were ones that never reached the Olympiads because they had lost their license.

The first victim of the Barr Body Test was the Polish sprinter Ewa Klobukowska. Klobukowska had a Barr Body in part of her cells. Having cells with two kinds of genetic makeup (with and without a Barr Body) means she is a "mosaic." Two kinds of cells are like different colored stones spread out over her body. This has consequences for your sexual development, for the sexual organs. Klobukowska has normal XX cells as well as cells with a Y-chromosome.

That DSD is a very complex syndrome, or rather a group of conditions, was proved by the Finnish geneticist Albert de la Chapelle. He offered his support to the aforementioned Mara Patiño. According to de la Chapelle, Patiño tested negative on the Barr Body Test and had no male traits at all.[32] Maria Patiño is completely insensitive to male hormones, so she couldn't have any benefit from a high level of testosterone. She did not have an unfair advantage over other female athletes, even though she has XY-chromosomes. De la Chapelle offered technical assistance to Patiño because he was a declared opponent of gender verification. According to de la Chapelle, gender verification was humiliating. He wrote that "it should stop."[33] Albert de la Chapelle wrote in the *Journal of the American Medical Association* in 1986 that the screening method used was "both inaccurate and discriminatory."[34] Patiño was barred in 1985 but got her license back in 1992. Alas, too late.

In 1992, the year that the IAAF stopped gender verification, the IOC introduced a new test. This test concentrated on a gene on the Y-chromosome called Sex Determining Region of Y, also know as the SRY-gene. So gender verification went from chromosomes to the more specific DNA. The SRY-gene codes for testicles. An embryo with a SRY-gene will develop testicles. It will be a baby boy. If the embryo has XX the indifferent gonads of the fetus will become ovaries.

After the testicles are formed, they release a cascade of hormones to take care of the rest of the sexual development. The sex is therefore determined by genes and hormones. This process starts in the seventh week of pregnancy. In the first six weeks all embryos look the same; there is no sexual development before the seventh week. But the embryo is, as it were, ready to develop in two ways, boy or girl. This is why men have nipples and why women have labia majora. The only period you were gender neutral was the time you spent as an embryo.

From 1992 until 1998 the IOC concentrated testing on this SRY-gene. At the Summer Games of 1996 eight young women tested negative, but they were all insensitive to testosterone and/or testicles had already been surgically removed. So in the end all eight got their license back.[35] Gender verification proved a failure once again, and there was so much protest from medical, genetic scientist and human rights organizations at the end of the last century, that the IOC gave in. Mandatory gender verification for all athletes was abolished in 1999 for all future Games, starting in Sydney 2000. So the Winter Games of Nagano in 1998 were the last Games with compulsory gender verification. In 1999 the IOC stopped mandatory testing but reserved the right to test individual doubtful cases—meaning that the IOC can request that individual contenders take such tests at any time, including an intensive evaluation by a gynecologist, a geneticist, an endocrinologist, a psychologist, and an internal medicine specialist. This brought us back to 1936 where individual suspect athletes were asked to visit a specialist.

In the first decade of this century several women were suspended, like the tragic case of Santhi Soundarajan, who tried to end her life by ingesting a pesticide. She couldn't keep it in, thankfully. She now owns a school for athletics in India.

In 2008 the aforementioned young African woman named Caster Semenya was secretly tested in Berlin, but the results were leaked to the press.[36] South Africa seethed with anger. Could this be sexist *and* racist? Nelson Mandela strongly stood behind his compatriot. The case of Semenya was another disgrace for sports. Once again the privacy of a woman was violated in a humiliating manner. It was high time for a change. It was high time gender verification stopped once and for all. But it didn't.

The IOC appointed a commission of scientists with the assignment to give advice on the future of gender verification. On the basis of this advice the IOC introduced a new set of rules for hyperandrogenic women.[37] Now the screening moved from DNA to hormones. The idea behind the new policy was the argument that testosterone "closes the gap between men and women." So a high level of testosterone was considered unfair in the female competition. The IOC agreed. Hyperandrogenic athletes should bring their T-level down to the usual female level. Then they would be eligible for the competition again. So from now on an athlete was not suspended for life, but could return to the competition after a hormone treatment or surgery.[38] That was a major step forward for intersex athletes.

There are two main methods to bring the T-level down: surgery or medication. Both treatments are medically unnecessary and have health risks. Caster Semenya chose to stay the person she was and followed the route of testosterone inhibitors or perhaps anti-conception medication. She brought her T-level down, became eligible for the Olympic Games and won the gold medal for the 800m in London. No big surprise because the testosterone had already done its job in puberty.

In 2015 the Indian hyperandrogenic 100m athlete Dutee Chand brought her case before the Court of Arbitration for Sport (CAS). Her argument was that there is no scientific proof that a high T-level gives the athlete a significant benefit. The court consulted scientists on the research on T-levels and sports performance and agreed with Chand. There was hardly any scientific research done on the role of endogenous testosterone in sports performance. There was only research done on synthetic testosterone, which has a different quality. The testosterone rules were suspended for two years to give the IAAF the opportunity to do their homework. In July 2017 the IAAF had to admit that the benefit was restricted to the middle distances, 400m to a mile.[39] Case closed, because Chand is a 100-meter athlete. Chand had won her case against the IAAF—a major win for a 19-year-old athlete.

But the IAAF opened the hunting season again and announced that hyperandrogenic athletes on the middle distances should bring their testosterone level down with a new, very strict cut-off. The IAAF announced this new regulation for the middle distances in November 2018.[40] Caster Semenya brought her case before the Court of Arbitration for Sport. She lost the case and an appeal at the High Court of Switzerland. She did not, however, intend to bring her T-levels down and concentrated on soccer and the 200-meter sprint.

The discussion up to now was a discussion of nature: DNA and hormones. Nurture has never been a subject of the arguments. Is the gap between boys and girls really just a matter of nature? After all, the assignment of sex at birth determines the manner in which a child is raised, and also determines their development.[41] In lay terms a boy throws a ball more effectively than a girl. And this might not be a result of nature, but the result of practicing in his youth.

A young girl—let's say she's 8—typically does not make any use of lateral space to throw. She does not stretch her arm sideward; she does not twist her trunk; she does not move her legs, which remain side by side. All she does in preparation for throwing is to lift her arm forward to the horizontal and to bend the forearm backward in a pronate position. The ball is released without force, speed, or accurate aim, precisely at the wrong moment.

A boy of the same age, when preparing to throw, typically stretches his right arm sideward and backward; supinates the forearm; twists, turns and bends his trunk; and moves the foot on his throwing side backward. From this stance, he can support his throwing almost with the full strength of his total motor skills. The ball leaves the hand with considerable acceleration; it moves toward its goal in a long flat curve.[42]

I'll bet there's no gene for throwing a ball on the Y-chromosome. It's a matter of practicing and of course interest. Boys get more practice because their parents give them more space to play. Girls are more often kept in the proximity of their parents and less encouraged to develop athletic skills. So boys practice a lot more physical skills in their youth. They play on the street, run, climb trees, play on sports-fields, like to show off, etc. This gives them an important head start for playing sports. (All this, of course, is culturally specific, and there are obviously exceptions.)

I throw like a boy and in the 1970s I learned to throw a frisbee with speed and great accuracy. I still can at 60, but underhand. My son attends a school where the frisbee is the mascot. Students are all provided with frisbees and compete with other schools in frisbee games. My son has learned to throw a frisbee in all sorts of ways, like overhand and sideways, even bouncing off the asphalt. I can't do this no matter how hard I try. I cannot seem to learn to throw a frisbee overhand, although it looks quite easy. Just a twist of the wrist at the right moment. To me that is a very complex motor skill. My son has a head start, I can never catch up. Boys learn motor skills at a young age and this may influence the development of the brain. Girls tend to have better fine motor skills than boys. Boys tend to have better motor and spatial skills, whereas girls tend to have a better verbal memory and social cognition.[43]

What I hope to illustrate with this little example: do not compare intersex girls with boys on the playing field. Intersex girls were raised as girls and were usually kept in the proximity of their parents. You just cannot say that if a girl refuses to abide by the testosterone rule, she has to compete with the boys. There's a lot more to being good at sports than having a high T.

Dora Ratjen

"Da sei etwas nicht in Ordnung"

In 1934, a delegation from the United States Olympic Committee paid a short visit to Nazi Germany.[1] The committee was chaired by Avery Brundage. The Games of 1936 were assigned to Berlin in 1931, but when Adolf Hitler was appointed as chancellor in 1933, the mood changed. Already in 1933, the first measures against Jews were being taken and Hitler was gaining more and more power. Confidence that the Games would proceed without anti–Semitism gradually sank in the U.S.

Avery Brundage's goal was to take the political and moral situation in Berlin into consideration. Brundage himself was an outspoken opponent of a possible boycott. "The Olympiad belongs to the athletes and not to the politicians" was his position.[2] Worldwide the call for a boycott was not widespread. There were a handful of athletes who personally refused to go. Some were Jewish, others liberal or socialists. But if you didn't go you wouldn't win a medal, and your name would get lost in sports history, even though morally you would be right not to go. You would be on the right side of history, but the winner takes it all.

Sadly for those athletes that stayed at home, there would be no opportunity to participate in the Olympics for another twelve years. The first Games after '36 were in London in 1948. There was no important international competition in between. So everybody knows Jesse Owens, but no one remembers Tollien Schuurman, world record holder of the 200 meters. She did not want to "run for Hitler and his accomplices."[3]

Eventually a total number of 49 countries took part in the Summer Games of Berlin, twelve countries more than four years before in Los Angeles. A historic number. If we could look back in innocence to the Games of 1936 we would say that these Games were a huge success for Germany and for the sporting world. In 1936 the press noted that the games were more successful than ever before.

In 1934 the call for a boycott was loud in the Jewish community in the U.S., the country with the largest delegation of athletes and a strong Jewish lobby—so strong that Brundage called it a "Jewish Communist conspiracy" against participation in the Games in Berlin.[4] He knew his classics. Brundage was, as we shall see, an anti–Semite himself.

Jeremiah Mahony, the president of the American Athletic Union, wanted a boycott because, according to him, Germany violated the Olympic Charter on discrimination by faith and race. The most important matter of principle for the Americans and the IOC was that German-Jewish athletes would not be excluded from participation in the Games. Hitler approved the participation of Jewish athletes from other countries. He had no choice. That was not the point. But would he approve Jews in the German teams?

Brundage announced after his visit to Germany that he had determined that the Jewish athletes would be treated fairly and that the Games should continue. The truth is that he made sure that just—as he said—"one Jew" would participate on the German team.[5] In other words, he was promised one Jewish athlete by the German committee. That athlete was the high jumper Gretel Bergmann.

The interlocutor for Brundage was Reichssportführer Hans von Tschammer und Osten.[6] The Reichssportführer was an SA leader and member of the Reichstag. The entire "sports atmosphere" fell under his leadership. Although Hitler saw sport as an elite activity for British snobs in the early 1930s, von Tschammer und Osten was highly motivated. Sports could make the mind and body stronger and the German athlete could experience being part of a larger national goal, he contended. In the 19th century the German nationalist Friedrich Ludwig Jahn—a high school teacher—proposed to make German boys and men more fit through gymnastics. The male population had been weakened by constant warfare and gymnastics was one of the answers to this problem. With friends he started a *Turnverein*, a gymnastics club, but it was not a sports club as we know them nowadays. The *Turnverein* was essentially a nationalist movement. Jahn's admirers called him their *Turnfather*, meaning patriarch of gymnastics. In 1816 he published his book *Der Deutsche Turnkunst*—the German art of gymnastics—and in this book he laid out his thought on sports and the upheaval of the German nation. His book is one of the first serious publications on sports. But Jahn was in a permanent conflict with the government, who saw his *Turnvereins* as political organizations. In 1823 Jahn was imprisoned for two years, but he eventually received an Iron Cross in 1840 for his bravery in the Napoleonic wars. Jahn even became a member of the German parliament. The Nazis of course celebrated father Jahn. So Hitler was easily convinced of the value of sports for uplifting the Aryan "race." But organizing the Olympic Games for that purpose was something else.

Joseph Goebbels, German minister of propaganda, saw the great potential of the Games for presenting Germany as a great and strong nation, a nation that knew how to organize such a great event.[7] Nazi Germany would be able to use the Games as means of propaganda. The Nazis aimed to promote a new, strong and united Germany by organizing the Olympics. So by 1936 Hitler had become a true sports fan, cheering on and showing sympathy for the teams that did or did not make it for Germany. In the film *Olympia: Fest der Völker,* made by Leni Riefenstahl, you can see Hitler showing enthusiasm but also disappointment as the German relay team loses the baton. Hitler visited the Games lots of times, congratulating winners and sharing his grief together with the German athletes. This is a part of the man we can hardly imagine. He did not congratulate the winners of the relay, but went straight to the German team to comfort them.

With only one exception in the Summer Games, no German athletes were Jewish. And the exception was not Gretel Bergmann, but a *Mischling* fencer, who had two Jewish grandparents. *Mischling* means "of mixed blood." In 1935 *Mischlings* were still *Reichsbürger,* lawful Germans according to the Nuremberg Laws.

In 1935 all German-Jewish athletes had been removed from their sports clubs and placed in Jewish-only clubs.[8] In September 1935, as the new laws became effective, the overarching German association for Jewish athletes, *Makkabi Deutschland,* pulled all its members out of the preliminary rounds for the Games, because of the virulent anti–Semitism. That was a great help to the Nazis, because now they did not have to make any effort to keep Jewish athletes on board. The Jewish boycott of the Games is very understandable; the German Jews had lost their civil rights in their own country. But one should keep in mind that this also applied for the black population in the U.S. They had hardly any rights and lived in their own districts, went to their own schools and joined their own associations. Jesse Owens in Berlin was happy to see that he could travel by bus without restrictions. He could go everywhere he liked; he saw no signs that said, "Whites only." He felt free in Berlin (for the Games the anti–Jewish signs had been removed from the streets, parks and sports facilities). The main difference between the U.S. and Germany was that African Americans were provided unlimited access to join an Olympic team.

Von Tschammer und Osten promised Brundage in writing that high jumper Gretel Bergmann would be part of the German team. Gretel Bergmann was ranked as one of the two best high jumpers in Germany. She belonged at the top of world lists with Elfriede Kaun. Dora Ratjen came in third.

Gretel Bergmann was born in 1914 in Laupheim in southwestern Germany. According to Nazi laws, she was a full Jew, being a Jewish woman with four Jewish grandparents. After she was forced to train in a Jewish club—Ulmer FV—with no facilities whatsoever, she decided to take up her studies in London. Under pressure of reprisal measures against her family, von Tschammer und Osten forced her to return to Germany. She became, as she said herself, the "alibi-Judin" of the Olympic Games. However, she did not yet suspect that the Reichssportführer did not intend to let her participate in the Games at all. She was indeed his alibi to reassure the Americans.[9]

As the SS *Manhattan*—the ship that brought the American team to Europe in June 1936—left the port of New York, Gretel Bergmann received a letter from the Reichssportführer that she was taken out of the Olympic team because of her "underperformance." He offered her a ticket for a standing place in the Olympic Stadium as a thank you for her efforts. The other jumpers, Kaun and Ratjen, were told that Bergmann was injured. Of course, they had never believed that underperformance could be the reason for her suspension. Bergmann had recently jumped 1.60 meters, matching the German record of Elfriede Kaun. Germany had two places in the high jump for females, and Bergmann and Kaun would under normal conditions have been assigned these two places.[10]

But Bergmann was barred. The Nazis were counting on the fact that once the Americans were on their way, they would not decline to participate in the Games. That was a correct assumption: The Americans did not even protest against the suspension of Bergmann. That should, of course, have been done. The Americans accepted the suspension without comment.

Gretel Bergmann had long since been replaced as the token Jew by the foil fencer Helene Mayer. Mayer was four years older than Bergmann and had won gold at the Games of Amsterdam at the age of 18, the youngest winner ever in her discipline. She was born in 1910 in Offenbach am Main. She too did not live in Germany, but in the U.S. Mayer was a *Mischling*, a woman with two Jewish grandparents, both on her father's side. Her father had died when Mayer was still a young child. Her mother did not keep in touch with her late husband's Jewish family. Helene Mayer was a fair blond woman. She was called "The Blond Hé" (Hé from Hélène). She used to wear her blond hair in braids, looking more Aryan than many Nazis. She was educated secularly at home and went to Christian schools. At the end of December there was always a Christmas tree in the Mayer house. Judaism meant nearly nothing to her; she did not feel connected to it. She loved her native country more than anything else. Being abroad she always longed for Germany, even after the war. In her pre-war days in the U.S. Mayer was lonesome and homesick. Thus, Mayer was very proud and eager to get the opportunity to represent her country in Berlin. She finished second and brought the Hitler salute on the podium, wearing a swastika on her jacket. Three Jewish girls (two *Mischlings*) won the medals. The Hungarian Ilona Elek took the gold, silver for Helene Mayer and bronze for Ellen Preiss from Austria. Preiss was born in Germany, but moved to Austria when she was 18. She had two nationalities but fenced for Austria. These three Jewish foil fencers are still seen as the best foil fencers in the history of the Olympic finals ever.

Fencing (and boxing), one could say, was a Jewish sport. In the 19th century Jewish students were often challenged to fight duels against non–Jewish students. It was a result of anti–Semitism for sure. And the sword was the weapon to fight these academic duels. So Jewish students took up fencing as a sport and a way of defending themselves in academic circles, getting better and better, and finally winning lots of medals at the Olympics. The list of Jewish elite fencers is long.

Mayer survived the war because she returned to the States after the Olympics. Imogen Cunningham took some stunning photographs of Mayer. But Mayer was homesick again. She returned to Germany in 1953, but died shortly after her migration of breast cancer, at just 43 years old. According to experts Mayer was the best foil fencer ever.

But not only the fencing finales were close, the high jump for women is also still seen as the most exciting finale ever, and was filmed by Riefenstahl.[11] This high jump final is also remembered by the participation of Dora Ratjen, who took the place of the suspended Gretel Bergmann. No

88888

one, including the Nazis, could at that time suspect that Dora Ratjen was a biological man. This was a man in masquerade, but he was no deceiver, although it was close. Ratjen was eventually 2 cm short of an Olympic medal.

Two years after the Games, in September 1938, Dora Ratjen jumped a new world record for women at the European Championships in Vienna: 1.67 meters. Vienna was at that time part of the German Reich. On his return trip to Bremen, a police doctor concluded that Dora Ratjen was a man. After that event Ratjen never spoke again about this shameful period in his life. In the vacuum that created, the wildest fantasies arose. And the conspiracy theory is always the theory that appeals to people the most. Behind every injustice is always a conspiracy for these imaginative thinkers. The conspiracy thinker suddenly understands the way things are. There are several conspiracy theories behind suspensions of intersex athletes. The banning of Ewa Klobukowska in 1967 was for the Poles a revenge of the Western Bloc against the Eastern Bloc. A plot was also theorized behind the suspension of the Dutch runner Foekje Dillema, involving a trap laid by her rival Fanny Blankers-Koen and her husband Jan Blankers. The truth is, of course, different and far more complex.

The conspiracy theory behind Dora Ratjen is as follows: The Nazis replaced Gretel Bergmann with a man dressed as a woman in order to secure the gold for Germany, but not by a Jew. Dora was the secret weapon of the Nazis. This theory was published after the war by *Time* magazine based on a conversation with a German bartender named Hermann. He claimed that Nazis had forced him into jumping in the female competition. It was fake news of the worst sort. The journalist had made it up and published a sensational article on one of the greatest frauds in sports history. The internet lives on these top tens of great sports frauds, though the stories often have little truth in them.

This conspiracy theory on Ratjen was also brought up in the successful film *Berlin '36* by Kasper Heidelbach.[12] The film claims to tell a "true story." In that story the Nazis placed a man on the German high jump team just before the start of the Games. The Nazis would have deliberately contributed to this deception. Ratjen—who is called Marie Ketteler in the movie— is forced by the Nazis to take Bergmann's place in the high jump. At the end of the film, Gretel Bergmann tells in persona that Dora was forced to play the game. Bergmann was convinced that the Nazis had played this trick on her. Bergmann, however, is little to blame. She had already read the fantasy story in *Time* magazine in the waiting room of her New York dentist and had burst out laughing. Now she understood why Dora behaved so mysteriously and why he always played hide and seek. Now she understood why the Nazis had set her aside. The penny had dropped, but it was a false penny.

The director and producer of the movie *Berlin '36* should have paid more attention, because the facts were already there. Stefan Berg, a journalist from *Der Spiegel,* had already published the official report and the correspondence on the arrest of Dora Ratjen.[13] Moreover, Professor Harmut Bosinski was prepared to open the medical files on Ratjen because he was convinced that you could not raise a boy as a girl. So what was Dora's true story?

Dora Ratjen was born on November 20, 1918, in a family with three daughters. The midwife determined that he was a boy, but changed her judgment ten minutes later. The child was a girl after all. The parents registered their daughter in the presbytery and in the municipality as Dora Ratjen.

Dora's parents owned a small bar in the village of Erichshof, near Bremen. They were simple people who relied on the advice of their general practitioner. It was not an easy judgment for the doctor either, because Dora suffered from hypospadias, a birth defect in which the urethra opens on the underside of the penis. "In some cases," writes the Dutch Association for Urology, "hypospadias can be so serious that it is not clear after birth whether it is a boy or a girl." In that case, a team of experts is immediately ready to support and treat parents and children: a psychologist, geneticist, an endocrinologist and a surgeon. But in the past a child with ambiguous sex characteristics was usually raised as a girl. That was the common advice. Severe hypospadias is regarded as an intersex condition.[14] But on the man-woman spectrum they are more on the male side than on the female side. The life story of Ratjen makes this quite clear.

Being raised as a girl was of course very difficult for these children, especially with all those hormones raging through their bodies during puberty, causing male secondary sex characteristics such as an Adam's apple, the lowering of the voice and facial hair. That also applied to Dora. He, too, had a very hard time. But how could you change your gender in the 1930s at the age of 15?

For some time after Dora's birth his father doubted the correctness of the sex choice. In the first year of Dora's life, he consulted the local doctor and told him: "da sei etwas nicht in Ordnung" ("this is not quite in order," or "something is wrong"). The doctor told him that there was nothing left to do: "Let it go, you cannot do anything about it." The parents were then resigned to the doctor's summary judgment. Dora's future was fixed. She would grow up as a girl, in girls' clothes, at girls' schools and at girls' sports clubs. Dora also had to accept his fate, although he often doubted himself that he should have to go through life as a girl, seeing as he was shaving every two days.

Dora not only lived with three sisters in the family, he also socialized with female friends only. Things became difficult at puberty. Dora did not develop breasts and had no menstruation, but shame stopped him from talking to others about it. He never undressed in the presence of the sports team. His teammates thought that the village girl was too shy for that. Dora lived a suffering double life; that was his fate.

In 1934 Dora became a member of athletics association *Vfb Komet* in Bremen and took up a job on the assembly line in the cigarette industry. Always surrounded by women, he also had to conceal his real gender there. He avoided occasions where people swam, danced or showered together. So no one noticed or even suspected that Dora was a man. Dora developed into a high jumper at *VfB Komet*. He wasn't good enough to compete as a man. In the men's competition, the bar was set 40 centimeters higher.

Germany prepared for the Games of 1936 and the Nazis were able to overcome their aversion to women's sport. This repulsion was pretty much universal. Opponents thought that sport had a negative influence on the fertility of women and German women's main role was to give birth to German children. It was during this feverish period that Dora became acquainted with the other two Olympic candidates: Elfriede Kaun and Gretel Bergmann. They later stated that they had no idea that the almost five years younger Dora was a man. "I had no idea," said Gretel Bergmann, "never."[15] The relationship of the three candidates was always relaxed and friendly. They were fine with each other. They also sometimes slept in the same room, about which Ratjen would later say that he had "never done anything that was unlawful."

Ratjen was 17 at the start of the Games in Berlin. He represented Germany together with Elfriede Kaun. It was a very exciting tournament. This contest goes down in history as the most exciting high jump finale ever. Three finalists jumped 1.60 meters. Only the British Dorothy Odam jumped flawlessly more than 1 meter 60. According to the regulations in 1936, there was a jump-off for the medals and the Hungarian Ibolya Csàk jumped 1.62.

Dora Ratjen

The altitude does not count officially because it was jumped in a jump-off, but she nevertheless got the gold. Dorothy Odam received the silver because she jumped a clear 1.60 and Kaun won the bronze. Dora became fourth at 1 meter 58.

The competition was captured by Leni Riefenstahl in the film *Olympia: Fest der Völker*.[16] You can feel the tension watching the competition. The high jump final can be seen on YouTube. We see Dora Ratjen jumping and Kaun intimately embraced by Ratjen. On the platform, Kauni—as the fans call her—brings the Hitler salute. Gretel Bergmann later asked her how she could be so naïve. "Politics did not interest me at all, I also maintained friendly contacts with Jewish athletes," Kaun said. Bergmann and Kaun continued to write each other throughout their lives.

Dora Ratjen continued his sporting life after the Olympic Games and took part in the European Championships in Vienna in September 1938. The world record he set in Vienna held for just two days, because on the way back to Bremen he was stopped by a train conductor. Dora was stretching his legs on the platform of the Magdeburg station at noon. The conductor was mistrustful. He reported to the police that there was a transvestite on the platform. This was forbidden in Germany in 1938. Ratjen was wearing a dark gray dress with gray pinstripe, skin colored stockings and ladies' sandals with a heel.

Inspector of police Sömmering looked closely at Dora and noticed how hairy his hands were. Dora showed him his sports card, but the inspector kept his doubts and escorted Ratjen off the train to the police station. There Sömmering threatened to investigate Dora himself. "What happens if I refuse?" asked Dora. The police officer answered that Dora would be detained. Dora then acknowledged that he was a man. He was then accused of fraud and the police took photographs of the athlete. In these, Ratjen can be seen dressed and undressed, still wearing his high heels. It was September 21, 1938. He was less than 20 years old and, according to the law, underage. And a man instead of a woman. In September 2009 the German journalist Stefan Berg published the story of the unmasking of the man Dora Ratjen in the magazine *Der Spiegel*: "How Dora the Man Competed in the Woman's High Jump."

The next day, Berg wrote, a police doctor arrived in Magdeburg and concluded that Dora's primary sex characteristics were unmistakably male. According to the doctor, Dora must therefore be regarded as a man, although there was a band of scar tissue running to the back of the penis, making it like a vagina. According to the doctor, it would therefore be difficult for Dora to have sexual intercourse. This scar tissue is also one of the possible explanations for the uncertainty about his gender at birth. "I was raised by my parents as a girl," Dora says in the official report.

Reichssportführer von Tschammer und Osten was informed and he ordered Ratjen's arrest. Ratjen was taken to Heilstätten Hohenlychen—a sports sanatorium—for further research. There they came to the same conclusion—to the relief of the person concerned. Finally, Dora had a clear answer to the question of whether he was a man or a woman. He had already begun to realize that he could not continue to live as a woman for much longer. Dora got new identification and became employed as a disabled worker in Hamburg. There was no judge involved. According to the prosecutor, he was no fraud; after all, he had never been told that he was a man, either informally or formally.

Stefan Berg concluded in the *Der Spiegel* article, after examining all the relevant documents—including the correspondence from the Reichssportführer—that there was no involvement of the Nazis in this somewhat tragic story. No indication has been found that there was a preconceived plan to commit fraud at the Games. The Nazis were just as surprised as everyone else. The editorial board of the German athletics association wrote in the magazine *Der Leichtathlet* that "Ratjen would no longer be admitted to the women's competition after a medical examination." Case closed.

No, not yet. Dora's father refused to change Dora's name and sex. Dora was a minor at the time and so the parents were tasked with the decision. His father wanted Dora to continue dressing as a woman because he "cannot pee standing." Moreover, the parents' bar was full of photos and trophies from their successful daughter. There was tremendous shame involved. Finally, a judge was called in and the official gender changed to "man." Dora's father gave in and asked the judge to change Dora's name to Heinrich. Heinrich promised never to play sports again.

Heinrich Ratjen took over his parents' bar after the war, but he refused to speak about the period when he lived his life as a girl. Ratjen sent his medals to the rightful winners and his records were removed from the record books. Heinrich Ratjen died in 2008. Elfriede Kaun died the same year; she was the longest living German medalist of the Games of 1936. High jumpers live longer!

The 1966 story in *Time* magazine about major sports scandals stated that Hermann (note the incorrect first name) Ratjen had confessed in tears that he had participated as an athlete at the Games for the honor and glory of Nazi Germany. He said that he had lived for three years as a girl and that was very boring. It is clear that *Time's* journalist never spoke with Heinrich Ratjen. But the story did lead a life of its own. These stories are persistent. They pop up every now and then, because they are sensational.

The final question is, of course: Was Ratjen's participation in the female competition fair play or unfair play? There are two sides to this question. First, the moral component: Did Ratjen deliberately falsify his gender to enter the competition? The second component of fair play is the question of an equal competition.

Whether Ratjen falsified his gender on purpose is a difficult question. On the one hand he lived his life as a woman and could not change his sex without bringing harm to his family and himself. Changing your sex this way would have been unprecedented. His face would have been on the covers of all popular papers and beyond. You can imagine the headlines: "Sports Girl Turns Out to Be a Boy." On the other hand he felt something was very wrong with his body: he had a beard, no breasts, and hair on his hands, arms and legs. He had his doubts.

The second question concerns equal opportunities in the competition. Although in truth, there are no equal opportunities, because then every jumper would jump the same height. But sports strives for equal opportunities by dividing the competition into male and female. And although for a man he was a mediocre high jumper, Ratjen held the world record in the female competition. This is most probably because he was male.

Foekje Dillema
"They say I'm not a girl"

As Foekje Dillema gathered her belongings from the train, her team-mates asked her what was wrong. Foekje answered, "They say I'm not a girl."[1] Without another word, she left the train, suitcase in hand, leaving her teammates behind in total bewilderment. After she had refused to participate in a mandatory gender verification, Dillema was stopped on her way to an international track meet to be held in Carcassonne, in the South of France. Board members of the Dutch Athletics Union took her aside and told her she was never allowed to compete in track again. After her death in 2007 it became clear why.

Being a rare name in the Netherlands, its origin being Frisian, when the name Foekje comes up, everyone knows you're talking about Foekje Dillema, the former 200 meters specialist. In the spring of 1950 Dillema was the fastest runner in the world in the 200 meters.[2] She was faster than her contemporary, Fanny Blankers-Koen, who was honored as best female athlete in the last century by the International Amateur Athletics Federation. Fanny Blankers-Koen had won the maximum amount of gold medals that could be won by a female in the 1948 London Olympics. She won four gold medals: two for sprinting events, and one each for the relay race and the hurdles. Fanny despised Foekje. "I do not run against men," she said.[3]

In August 1950 the athletes were required to bring a certificate—acquired in each athlete's native country—to the European Championships. It was to be signed by a gynecologist confirming that the athlete was female. The certificate—the so-called sex certificate—was to be presented by the athlete at the meeting held in Brussels, Belgium. Without this certificate athletes were not allowed to compete in the female competition. This procedure was mandatory for all athletes, even if they had birthed children, as

Fanny Blankers-Koen had. There was no exception, although there was no official ruling that said you had to be female for the female competition.[4]

Officially the certificate was to eliminate "men in masquerade" from the female competition; unofficially we know the tests were aimed at the so-called "hermaphrodites." Hermaphrodites were seen as men in masquerade by the international unions.

The Dutch Athletic Union was very eager to help the IAAF with its new cause, because they thought Foekje Dillema was a "hermaphrodite"— an athlete with aspects of both sexes. Board members of the Dutch union referred to her as a "kween" (queen), a derogatory word for intersex goats.[5] Some, like Fanny Blankers-Koen, even thought she was a man,[6] meaning she would have been a fraud. But was she? This is a rhetorical question of course.

The British runner Sylvia Cheeseman told me in 2019 that she had forgotten all about the gender verification and confirmed that she had to visit the academic hospital in Brussels in August 1950 just before the championship. The doctors in the hallway had a big laugh at such a strange request, and signed the certificate without a physical examination. The Dutch girls, however, couldn't get away with such ease. They were expected at the Westeinde Ziekenhuis (hospital) in the Hague on Saturday, July 8, 1950.[7] The late Dutch runner Puck Brouwer told the press in 2004 she had to "take [her] place in a gynecological examination chair, spread her legs, and the spotlight was on."[8] This was a humiliating experience for a young woman of 19 years.

The same day of the examinations, the Dutch Athletic Union gathered for a meeting in Hotel Terminus, Utrecht. Although the complete archive of the Dutch Athletic Union from that period was destroyed, in 2010 the minutes of this meeting were found in the attic of Bart Kappenburg, a former board member. The minutes state: "Foekje Dillema cancelled the examination. Tonnis de Vries will contact her if necessary."[9] Apparently Foekje Dillema had written a letter to the board explaining that she was not going to attend the mandatory verification. Tonnis de Vries was the coach of the Dutch track team and would meet with her on the following Wednesday evening. Foekje ran with the Dutch relay team that same Wednesday evening in Groningen City Park. The next day Foekje Dillema was ordered out of the train to France and expelled for life from competition.[10] What had happened? We don't know what was discussed between Foekje and coach de Vries, but without a doubt Foekje had persisted in her refusal to go to the examination, as evidenced by her being ejected from the train the next day. In the early morning of this dark day, July 13, 1950, the Union had sent Foekje a telegram (there was no phone in the Dillema household), which arrived after Foekje had left the house on her bicycle for the nearest railway station in Buitenpost.[11] The board members never expected her to be on the train. That they were mad as hell can be expected. What did they know? And what could she do about it? Miscommunications led to a lot of anger and fear. Who was she?

Like almost all intersex athletes, Foekje Dillema was born in a village in a rural community. My hypothesis is that amenorrhea—absent menstruation—is not discussed in rural families and therefore their intersex condition remains unnoticed even through adolescence. It's the predominant shame culture in most rural areas. Most mothers in other areas take their daughters to a hospital for a gynecological examination. In rare cases experts like geneticists and endocrinologists may conclude that the girl has no uterus, and today they can conclude that the girl has no ovaries, but internal testes instead. They perform a chromosome test to diagnose the cause of the condition.

According to her elder sister Aafke Dillema, Foekje did not menstruate[12]—"There was never anything in the bucket from Foekje"—and Aafke stated that this fact could not be discussed with their mother. Everybody knew, but no one talked about it.

Foekje was born on September 26, 1926, in the very small village of Burum in the northern province of Friesland, the Netherlands. Just two streets crossing each other. She was the third girl. As per rural tradition in those days, the first two girls were named after the parents of Foekje's father. Then the parents of the mother take their turn. The names of the children were reserved before they were born. Foekje was named after her mother's father. His name was Foeke, for which the female version is Foekje, literally meaning "little Foeke." The family lived together with this grumpy grandfather. Grandfather Foeke did not care about the first two children, who were named after the father's parents. Aafke, the oldest daughter, called it "name sickness," so it was no wonder that in her eyes grandfather Foeke was a grumpy man. It's as if the grandchildren that bear your genes are the only ones that are important.

Foekje lived in a cramped house: two rooms and a sleeping attic. Three sisters slept in one bedstead. In the end the family would consist of eight children. The fifth child was finally a boy, and he was also named after his grandfather Foeke. This meant that there was not only a Foekje, but also a Foeke, in the Dillema family. This proves that Foekje was not a boy initially called Foeke as was sometimes presumed. People falsely assumed that a boy named Foeke had participated as a male imposter under the name of Foekje.

Foekje's father, Pieter Dillema, never had a real job in his life. He was always unemployed due to one economic crisis after another and the war. He was sent out to work in land reclamation during a dark period in Dutch history. It was forced labor and only the shareholders of the new land earned any money from it. The workers were paid less than minimum wage. So the Dillema household was very poor. They could not afford to rent a house. And even in this worrisome situation it was unthinkable that the mother would take a job. Foekje's parents were very conservative. Mothers did not work for a living, they took care of the household. Of course many thousands of families were living in poverty in the 1930s. In spite of it all Pieter Dillema was a kind little man, who never complained. In the weekends he was always in the fields, gathering lapwing eggs, catching moles, skating in winter and fishing in summer. The girls loved to accompany their father on his trips.

Fortunately, grandfather Foeke brought in money from his trade in gasoline for kitchen stoves. The gender roles were steadfast in this rural village. Mother Sybrigje took care of the children and the house. She was always behind the stove or her sewing machine. The machine had a central role in the living room. It was the most expensive tool in the house. A sewing machine was like a dowry, a bare necessity. All the girls had to learn how to sew and Foekje spent hours behind the machine to sew clothing for her siblings. When the famous Dutch photographer Ben van Meerendonk visited the family, he photographed Foekje doing women's activities like sewing, cooking, shopping and sometimes playing with the little village kids in the street.

Looking at these pictures you might assume that the photographer had a specific instruction to make a genuine girl out of her in order to refute all rumors of her being a man. On the other hand, it really was what Foekje did at home. She wasn't roaming the streets with the boys. She was kept in the proximity of her house. When Foekje was a young girl there was not much time for anything other than the household and school. Girls were preparing for their future role as mother and housekeeper. There was no time or money for sports or fun. A very sober youth, she spent her younger years just like any girl in a rural area would in those days; helping her mother peel potatoes in the kitchen, washing and sewing clothes when needed. She could always be found at home when not in school or at Sunday church and Sunday school, again behind the sewing machine "to help the poor."

Foekje never played sports during her childhood, although children in the village later remembered that she always won the summer street school races on national celebrations like Koninginnedag (Queen's Day—celebration of the queen's birthday). It was not until 1948 that she took up gymnastics.

Foekje always lived with her parents. She was socially handicapped and rather rude according to one nephew.[13] She was not suited for a job away from home. She said things a decent girl was not allowed to say. Her family thought she was a somewhat odd girl.

Foekje passed her first gender test—the test all newborn babies have to bear. She was declared a girl. Nobody in the family ever noticed anything different about her. Every Saturday the children would bathe together in the tub so they would have noticed of course if Foekje was a boy. But she wasn't.

Foekje always dressed as a girl and woman throughout her life although she was the kind of lady that looked better in trousers. She was very feminine and old fashioned in her way of dressing and only wore trousers on the track. In later life she always wore a scarf as if to state explicitly, "I'm a woman." By then she never left home without a scarf. None of her sisters wore scarves unless they went to church.

Puberty must have been a terrible period for Foekje. We can only imagine how lonely she must have been, not being able to talk about her troubles. Of course she would have liked to get married and have children. She adored children. Would she have been able to have them? This must have been one of the worries in her mind. It turned out Foekje was hyperandrogenic; her voice became deeper in puberty, hair started growing on her body and cheeks as a result of the elevated level of testosterone—and she would or could never talk to anybody about this. She became a tall, strong girl, with male secondary sex characteristics.

Puberty is the period of time where intersex conditions become apparent, for boys as well as for girls. XX boys will not reach puberty, because their testosterone level is too low. The testes are small and underdeveloped. XY girls will never menstruate because they have no ovaries. Not reaching puberty isn't a bliss for parents, it's a worrisome period. Their child has a disorder of sex development, they cannot live a normal live.

Too little hormones for boys, too much for girls. There will be no solace in sports. Unless of course the hyperandrogenic girl will be accepted without restrictions.

The Second World War took all the fun away in daily life for Dutch children. Their freedom of movement became restricted and no one was allowed to leave the house after dark. The houses were darkened against airstrikes. The young men were forced to work in Germany. People sought solace in watching sports games, like soccer.

I don't think Foekje had a happy youth. Maybe that was the reason for her being grumpy and quiet. She never talked much at home. Foekje was a quiet, lonely girl in a small village, surrounded by too many people in a small house. When the war came to an end, things changed for Foekje. Her sisters left the house one after another at an early age. After finishing school at the age of twelve, they went on to work full-time as maids. Little Cinderellas, but their lives were no fairy tale with delicate shoes and princes all over the place. They were lucky if the master of the household or his sons kept his hands off them.

Not too much later, the girls would get married and have children. Their lives were planned before they were even born. Aafke Dillema, the eldest sister, remembered the day her brother Mient was born. She was seventeen and felt yet another sibling was too much for her to handle, so she left the family home: "I just did not want to see him."

Foekje was not able to work as a maid in another family because of her social handicap, so she took a job as a cleaning lady at the age of twelve. She stayed with her parents, but there was more time for recreation after the war was over. She joined a gymnastics club called *Vlugheid en Kracht* (Speed and Strength) located in the neighboring village of Buitenpost. Gymnastics was the best way for girls to meet other boys and girls. In those days gymnastics was very popular in the Netherlands.

Her gymnastics teacher noticed she was a fast sprinter and advised her to join an athletic club.[14] Before deciding to join, Foekje asked to participate in the local sprint event for girls. She took off her shoes and, barefooted, beat all the other girls with ease. Keeping in mind that the girls she ran against were trained, the best from her province, Foekje then knew she would go in for running.

In 1947 Foekje joined the athletics club *Vitesse* in Leeuwarden, about 30 kilometers from her village. The track was on an ice rink, a grass track. Everyone called it the "cold track." There was only a shed to get dressed in, with no shower or running water, but as it was just after the war, nobody complained.

Foekje became a different person on the track. She talked, laughed and joked around with the other runners. Geesje Jorna, a teammate, remembered her as a brat, always joking around. Foekje's family wouldn't have believed it was their Foekje.[15] She had finally found her own place in life. Finally, she was good at something. She was the best and yet at home she was still the old quiet, closed-off girl. She hardly talked about her track training at home. She would only experience this happiness for the relatively short period of three years, then she was disqualified. Just three years, but they were the most important three years of her life. She traveled the country, went to London, thousands of people watching from the stands the day she beat the Italian relay track team in Rotterdam.

At Foekje's funeral in December 2007 the church minister talked about these years and even some close family members told me afterwards they never realized that their aunt had been the best 200-meter runner in the world. They never knew that thousands of people had watched her in the Olympic Stadium in Amsterdam and in 1949 at Whitehall in London.

After Foekje joined *Vitesse* things progressed quickly. Her coach tried to improve her starting technique, which was her weakest point. Foekje relied on the second 100 meters to outrun the other girls. That's why they called her the "Steam Engine." She might have made a good 800-meter runner. But after the first 800 finale in the Olympics of 1928, the distance was removed from the Olympic program. Some say the runners were exhausted crossing the line; others say the girls were very disappointed that they lost the race. Some of the girls fell into the grass in need of medical attention. One of the runners fainted in the locker room. The officials, all men, thought that they were right in their prejudice concerning women athletes. Lina Radke, who won the race, was very disappointed that the 800 meters event was eliminated. It wasn't until 1960 when women were allowed to run this distance again. This also meant that Radke held the Olympic title for 32 years. A lot has been said and written on the Olympic 800 meters in Amsterdam.[16] But it still remains rather mysterious.

Foekje Dillema was a very strong girl, but her hips were locked as she ran, and she threw her head back in the final meters. In fact, technically she did almost everything wrong that could be done wrong, but in the end she finished first. And that's what it's all about. Naturally she improved her technique in the first year, training in the Frisian team. Even if you're fast, there's a lot to learn. Her coach remembered her as a nice girl with a deep voice and hair on her cheeks.[17] But he never doubted her gender. No one did in Friesland, although she never partook in the communal showers with the other girls. They all thought that she was just a shy girl from a small village with no shower at home.

Fanny Blankers-Koen, however, was suspicious, according to the sports editor Klaas Peerenboom of *Het Parool*. She spied on her rival, looking through pinholes in the dressing room. "Maybe," she said, "maybe I saw a little penis," but she wasn't sure. She told the press that her husband made her spy on Dilemma.[18] This story wasn't published, of course. Reporters didn't write on these things. But the journalists discussed the situation among themselves speculating whether Foekje was a woman or a man. Fanny Blankers-Koen wasn't a very likeable woman. Even her daughter said so at her mother's funeral in 2004.[19] Fanny was a sore loser, she just couldn't lose, not even to her grandchildren. An old Dutch lady called me one day and she told me she had been a good sprinter as a child but eventually made a choice for ballet. She won every sprint. She remembered that in one race the daughter of Fanny Blankers-Koen participated and lost. Fanny took her aside and was raving mad at her daughter for losing the match.[20] This behavior comes as no surprise. "She always wanted to cycle away first at the traffic lights," her granddaughter said in a newspaper story. In these little details we meet the woman who was called the "flying housewife." The flying housewife was just a cliché to tell us that she was foremost a mother and second a runner—how it should be in the 1950s—though she was never really close to her children. She was a cold mother, according to her daughter. The image of the flying mother was incorrect.[21] But of course the Athletic Union did everything to protect this image.

Fanny (almost) never lost a match. Before the war she was selected for the national team going to the Olympics in Berlin. She replaced Tollien Schuurman, who refused to go because of the Nazis. Fanny Koen was just 18 years when she went to Berlin. The Nazi games made a big impression on her. She did not win any medals in 1936; she was too young and didn't have any professional training. She competed against several intersex athletes, like the high jumper Dora Ratjen and sprinter Stella Walsh. The war then ended all international competition.

During the war she married the police officer Jan Blankers. Jan was a former triple jump athlete who limped because of an unsuccessful jump.

Jan was 14 years older than Fanny. The pair had two children during the war: Jan and Fanny.

Jan the husband was a very authoritarian man. Jan Blankers was the coach of the women's team in Berlin 1936, the coach of his future wife. However, the girls never saw him. He visited the most exciting games at the Olympics and did not care a bit about female athletics. To him all the female athletes had deep voices and hair on their chins. He was not the right man at the right place but who cared? His pupils were "just" females. The team filed a complaint to the Dutch Union on his behavior. It had no effect, of course. All the board members were brazen misogynists. They just had a good laugh on the female athletes. The athletes didn't bring any medals back home. How could they? They were superfluous. There was no attention, nobody cared about them. The girls themselves were quite mad of course, but what could they do? This all changed for Jan Blankers after he married Fanny and became her personal trainer in her private athletics club by the name of *Sagita* (arrow), with just one active member, Mrs. Blankers.

Fanny said in later life that she owed everything to Jan. She grew very dependent on him, as if she were his daughter and not his wife. Jan trained his wife in wartime. Blankers himself worked with the Amsterdam police, a force that was very active in transporting Jews to Westerbork, a transit camp to Auschwitz. Jan Blankers was also the personal trainer of the SS officer Tinus Osendarp. Osendarp was called the fastest white man in the world, because he came in third in the sprint at the 1936 Olympics, finishing after Jesse Owens and Ralph Metcalfe. He was also a police officer and worked with the SS command Leemhuis in the Hague, dedicated to rounding up resistance fighters. One day in 1944 one of the captives escaped from Osendarp's car. Osendarp got out of the car and shot the resistance fighter in the back. After the war, during his trial, the judge wanted to know why the fastest white man in the world didn't sprint to catch him. Osendarp got 12 years imprisonment. After his punishment he became a mine worker and lived a quiet life.[22]

When Osendarp ran in the Olympic Stadium in his SS sports shirt during the war nobody cheered, and some even catcalled. The Nazis were mad as hell and all the spectators had to show their Ausweis (ID) before leaving the stadium. It took hours before the last spectator had finally left. The spectators were of course proud of their behavior. They hated Osendarp and loathed his collaborating coach Jan Blankers. Blankers, like all the other sports officials, didn't care much for politics. The Games had to go on, under any circumstances. I don't think Jan Blankers was on the wrong side in war-time, but he wasn't exactly on the right side either.

During the war the Nazis forced all local athletics clubs to join the Dutch Athletic Union. To the great delight of the Dutch Athletic Union, because this signified an end to all quarrels between clubs. And, of course, Jews were expelled from all Dutch clubs.[23] The Nazis wanted to control the sports clubs. Not all clubs were willing to join the Union but they were forced to. Clubs didn't want to because board members had joined the NSB, the Dutch national socialist party.

After the war, the Dutch Athletic Union had to be purified. It was a process that took five years. The president made up a story that he had helped the Canadians to liberate the south of the Netherlands. Initially, everybody believed him. Decades later historians found out that he had lied, he had got all the dates and places wrong. The president of the technical commission, Jo Moerman, had been a member of the NSB, but he was deemed indispensable for Dutch athletics. Moerman got away with only a one-week suspension. Five years later he suspended Foekje Dillema for life. These men could do almost anything they wanted, it seems.[24]

Jan Blankers stopped working for the police in 1949. He became the new editor-in-chief of sports news for the Dutch newspaper *Telegraaf*. The newspaper desperately needed journalists. Blankers had written a hand-book on athletics and knew everything there was to know, so the paper hired him. The *Telegraaf* had been a Nazi paper during the war and was out of print for four years after the war by authority of the government. "You just didn't want to work for this paper," said Blankers' former colleague from other newspapers to me.[25] They despised Jan Blankers. There was no communication whatever between journalists of the *Telegraaf* and journalists from other newspapers. After the war everything was defined in moral terms of right and wrong. There was nothing in between right and wrong. There was no grey between black and white. The newspaper had been on the wrong side. Most board members of the national athletic union had been on the wrong side. Thus, many clubs left the union again after the war.

But Jan Blankers was a very good trainer-coach. He even learned Swedish to read the best trainer's guides in the world. Fanny made a big impression in London 1948; with four gold medals she was the best female athlete of the century, together with the male laureate Jesse Owens. In 1952 Fanny wanted more gold medals in Helsinki. She was hindered by a nasty boil that was treaded badly by the team doctor, who was an eye doctor, by the way. And a child abuser. He was sentenced before the war, but nevertheless accepted as union physician. It took the members of the Dutch Athletic Union four years to get rid of him. So this was the circle of people who wanted Foekje out of competition.

Fanny refused to run against "Mister Dillema" as she called Foekje, and she never did on the 200-meter sprint. Foekje was, of course, disappointed in Fanny; she wanted the competition. The press was also disappointed in Fanny, but the Athletic Union stated that both women had to be spared for the major competitions in Europe. The Dutch public wanted so much to see Fanny against Foekje, the best sprinters in the world. Where did it start?

On June 21, 1948, Foekje ran her first official event, the 100-meter sprint, in Friesland. The referees couldn't believe their eyes when they looked at their stopwatches. The time could not be correct for a debut. So they readjusted her time down to 12.7 seconds, fast enough for a first appearance on the track. Even after the adjustment, those 12.7 seconds promoted Foekje to the first class. The Frisian press wrote, "Only her dark curls remind you of a woman. She could easily be a strong Frisian boy." This wasn't meant to be rude, there was no real suspicion then. The dark curls were by the way fake. From her first paycheck she went to the hairdresser. She always used to perm her hair.

The press drew a comparison to another Frisian female athlete, Tollien Schuurman. Schuurman was the first woman to break 12 seconds on the 100 meters. She was the greatest prospect to succeed at the 1932 Olympic Games in Los Angeles. Unfortunately, everything went wrong for her. False starts made Tollien insecure, and Stella Walsh won the gold medal. In 1936 Schuurman refused "to run for Hitler and his henchman," which prompted the Dutch Athletics Union to ban her for life.[26] "We always talked about politics at home," she told the press later. Her father was one of the first socialists in her district. President of the Athletic Union Strengholt even personally went to visit Schuurman to persuade her to go. She refused and was banned for life.[27] Tollien Schuurman is totally forgotten because she never won a great international match. Not running for Hitler meant guts but no glory.

In the spring of 1949 Foekje won all there was to win in the 100- and 200-meter events. Fanny Blankers-Koen avoided running against her, using all sorts of excuses. The public wanted to see a confrontation between "F & F" as they were called. This moment finally came on Olympic Day, in August 1949, a day devoted to raising money for the Olympic team in preparation for the 1952 Helsinki Games. Foekje was dealing with an injury, one that Fanny knew about, and she had consequently beaten Foekje during the 100-meter sprint. Even without the injury and Foekje still being a slow starter, she would have never been able to beat Fanny on the 100. Foekje was a 200-meter sprinter, a slow starter but fast finisher. Foekje cancelled her participation in the national championships and Fanny went on to win all the races with no pretext. In July 1949 the Frisian relay team became Dutch champions. This is the only title the Dutch Athletic Union forgot to erase from Foekje's honors.[28]

Foekje got her international breakthrough in September 1949, at the end of the athletic season, in White City Stadium in London. Fanny had chosen to stay home, saying she was "celebrating her son's birthday." Foekje's family had never left the country and of course Foekje didn't like the English food, but at least she could compete against a very strong runner named Sylvia Cheeseman, "the smiling athlete." Cheeseman was warned that there "was a man on the Dutch team." Cheeseman told me in 2008: "I just couldn't get away from all these men."[29] I told her that Foekje had lived with a complex intersex condition and Cheeseman gained considerably more respect for her. Foekje had beaten her in White City in the 100-meter and the 200-meter sprints. She earned the title Athlete of the Match and received a beautiful gold leaf. After her death all gold and bronze medals were stolen from the family. So it goes.

In May 1950 Dillema was selected for the national team. If Fanny wouldn't run against her, then they could always run together. Once in a fortnight Foekje would train in Amsterdam, together with her coach, Tonnis de Vries. The team planned to go on a trip to Carcassonne for a match between England, France and the Netherlands. But before this event there was the second Olympic Day in June 1950. As usual, Fanny refused to run against Foekje, but there was always the clock to run against and that day Foekje ran a new Dutch record on the 200 meters, finally beating Fanny Blankers-Koen's record.[30] It was Dillema's finest hour. She had become the world's fastest runner in the 200-meter sprint. Her record time was 24.1 seconds. Fanny was not amused. Two weeks later Foekje was banned for life. Her national record was erased and never reinstalled.

The IAAF started their first gender verification for the European Championships on August 23, 1950, in Brussels. Foekje refused to go to the hospital for her certificate and was expelled. Nobody dared to write about such things as gender. The fact that Foekje had refused to go was not made public and it was not until 2010 that sports historians found the minutes of the meeting of the Dutch Union. For sixty years nobody knew what had happened in 1950. Was Foekje a man, a woman, a hermaphrodite, or a mannish woman? There was the usual conspiracy theory that Jan and Fanny Blankers-Koen had tricked her into a gender verification. All of the Dutch girls in the national team were ordered to go to the hospital, and this whole scene was aimed at only one girl. The other girls were used as a cover-up. This was not true. The verification was organized by the IAAF. In later years journalists came to Foekje's door with questions but they were all sent away. In the end, almost everybody forgot about the athlete with the dark curls.

I started my research on the "case" about two years before Foekje died. As a sports historian, I wanted to get to the bottom of this enigmatic story. I spoke many times with Aafke, the eldest sister, and several specialists like the human geneticist Thirza Kraaijenbrink and the very helpful endocrinologist Prof. Dr. Wilma Oostdijk. Just after Foekje's death Aafke gave me the key to the solution; Foekje had her glands operated on at the Academic Hospital in Groningen not long after she was expelled from competition. Nobody in the family was allowed to visit her in hospital or to talk about the operation. It was a family secret. Foekje's mother got very irritated when the other children wanted to know what was wrong with their sister. With the help of medical advisors we came to the conclusion that the surgery must have been a gonadectomy, the surgical removal of testes. Foekje must have had a Y-chromosome. With no menstruation, a high T (resulting in facial hair) and a suspension from the female competition without protest, there could be no other conclusion. The testes were probably palpable in her groins. On the outside she was a woman, on the inside, not. I was quite satisfied with the conclusion, but Dutch television wanted to be sure when they were working a documentary on Foekje Dillema.

To test my theory, old pieces of clothing once belonging to Foekje were brought to the forensic lab at the Erasmus Hospital in Rotterdam. Skin cells were obtained from the inside of her dresses. Dead cells, even broken ones, could still contain enough DNA for analyses. The forensic researcher Kay Ballantyne did indeed find DNA fragments (markers) from the Y-chromosome. The chromosomes cannot be seen in dead cells; you have to rely on the DNA fragment. The hypotheses was right—Dillema had a Y-chromosome. So why wasn't she an XY-man then? Why was she born and raised a girl? Because the forensic researcher saw an unusual genetic pattern: there were more X than Y chromosomes in the skin cells.[31] The majority of female X-chromosomes had disordered her sex development. More X than Y is a very rare condition. The sex chromosomes should be balanced: XX for female, XY for a man. XXY or maybe even XXXY is an imbalance in sex chromosomes, causing all sorts of gender problems. So how does this get to be?

The first cell of Foekje Dillema was XY[32]: X inherited from her mother, Y from her father. The first cell was programmed to become a man. But the cell division did not go according to mother nature's plan. During cell division, all the chromosomes make copies of themselves, then are ordered on line in the middle of the cell. The two chromosomes and their copies are attached to each other in the middle, so just before division the copied pair looks like the letter X. Rope-like strands then pull one member of each pair to the opposite ends of the dividing cell. The mother cell divides into two daughter cells with the same genetic make-up. This is the heartbeat of life. But in Foekje's first cell the X-chromosomes did not separate. This is called non-disjunction. So then there is a daughter cell with XXY and a daughter cell with one Y-chromosome. The cell with just the Y-sex chromosome dies, because every cell needs an X to be viable. So after the first cell division there remained just the one cell with sex chromosomes XXY.

Ballantyne suggested that Dillema was XX and XY, as there might have been more non-disjunctions. XX/XY is a very rare condition: one in 40,000, and most of these pregnancies end in a miscarriage. But once in a while a child with this genetic make-up is born. So a part of her cells would be XX, the other part XY. This condition is called mosaic, because the different cells are scattered over the body as different stones in a mosaic. We don't know whether this conclusion is right. There are other possibilities. We just don't know. In order to see the genetic make-up, you need living cells, and Foekje had already died months before the DNA analysis. A chromosome test is done during cell division, because that's the moment you can color, see and count the chromosomes.

So as predicted after the conversations with Aafke Dillema, there was a Y-chromosome demonstrated in Foekje Dillema's DNA. The SRY-gene on this Y-chromosome codes for testes. With enough Y in the gender-neutral glands of an embryo, the glands will become testicles. But in a majority of X-chromosomes the sex development is then disordered. The child will not fully develop into a male, as we have seen in Klinefelter men with XXY-cells. Klinefelters have small, infertile testes. More X than Y leads to a DSD, Disorder of Sex Development. Foekje was, in scientific jargon, phenotype woman, genotype male. Woman on the outside but with a male chromosome. No ovaries, no menstruation. In the case of Foekje Dillema the internal testes made her hyperandrogenic; she had a high testosterone level, causing a deep voice, unwanted body hair and strong muscularity. But was it enough to become unbeatable on the track?

It was a sad and lonely life for Foekje after the IAAF banned her from competition. She didn't dare to leave her house for at least a year. It was a very shameful situation with people speculating about her gender all the time. The Dutch federation told the press that "due to a medical condition Foekje would never be able to compete again." We know from the local newspapers that after the suspension she skated (speed skating) and won several prizes. But speed skating on an international level was not allowed for ladies until 1960 in the Netherlands. Otherwise it would have been wiser for Foekje to become a speed skater, with no gender verifications. Without tragedy.

She was in her later life an enormous sports fan and watched all the games on television and later travelled the country with her young nephew Foeke to visit many games. No matter what the sport, from soccer to motor racing. Always a stoic in her long black leather coat and scarf, she spoke to no one. Tymen Wierstra wrote: "I still remember Foekje Dillema. She came regularly at the first of Kollum when I was about fifteen years old. There she stood, all alone in a long, black leather coat to watch the game like a stoic statue."[33] Many people remember Foekje with that long black leather coat and the scarf. And anytime Fanny Blankers-Koen was on the television, Foekje threw anything at hand to the screen, mostly the alarm clock. Even she held Fanny responsible for the tragedy.

Foekje worked all her life as a cleaning lady, and was loved by all the old folks she took care of. She gave sporting instruction to the youth of the village as a volunteer. She had learned so much from her own coach.

Not a day must have gone by for Foekje without thinking about that dark day in July 1950 when she was left all alone on the platform, watching the train depart for France. She would have wanted so much to be on board with her friends, to take part in the match. She boarded the train back to Friesland and made the longest and loneliest journey of her life back home. There was no after care. Just a train ticket back home.

Foekje died on December 5, 2007. I never spoke to her in the last years of her life, knowing her reputation of sending all journalists away. She didn't want to be bothered about her tragic past. And I did not want to bother her either. I went to her funeral, which was only attended by family and some people from the village. There were no other journalists, no official from the Dutch Athletic Union. Just one former athlete of her athletic days, Geesje Jorna. Geesje and Foekje had remained friends on Foekje's strict condition to never speak about the past. They never did. I was the only visitor from outside the village. Dillema was forgotten until I brought her to life again in a Dutch book on her life story.

The final goodbye was in the small sports facility of the village. The gymnastics ring was pulled up to the ceiling, and this resembled the five Olympic rings. It must have been pure coincidence. Foekje was buried alongside her parents, Sybrigje and Pieter Dillema, the people she had lived with all their lives and taken care of in their final years.

The funeral guests assumed that I was the son of Fanny Blankers-Koen, coming to make excuses. I had to disappoint them and told the family I wanted to write her biography. This was to their great surprise and delight. But I couldn't write the book they wanted to read. They had believed, as so many other people had, that Foekje had been betrayed by the competition. They had never doubted the gender of Aunt Foekje. Still, I wanted to write the truth, for the sake of many other intersex athletes. Suspension had to be stopped one way or the other and maybe the biography of one of the victims could clarify the humiliation the intersex athletes had to bear. I wanted to show that their lives had been ruined by immoral decisions and false notions on gender and hormones.

In 2018, ten years after Foekje had died, the IAAF published an article on the benefits of elevated levels of testosterone in female athletes.[34] One of the conclusions was that sprinters in the 100 and 200 meters do not benefit from a high T-level. This makes me think it is high time to restore Foekje's performance records in track and field to take effect retroactively, but I doubt it will ever happen.

A few weeks after her death I visited the family. Together we opened a cardboard box that been in her attic for years. In the box we found pictures from her days on the track. We found a book written by Jan Blankers on training methods for athletics. Knowing how she hated him, she must have closed the box in 1950 and never opened it again. We also found two books on the Olympics of 1948. Obviously going to Helsinki in 1952 must have been her biggest dream. But it turned into a nightmare two years earlier.

Ewa Klobukowska
One Chromosome Too Many

After the Polish sprinter Ewa Klobukowska was barred in 1967 based on a chromosome test, the IAAF informed the press that she had "one chromosome too many."[1] Only experts would have known, in the 1960s, that having "one chromosome too many" meant the Y-chromosome. Surely there's nothing wrong with an extra X-chromosome for a female. An extra X has no serious consequences and there would be no reason at all to suspend an athlete with XXX-chromosomes from the female competition. It's the Y-chromosome that counts.

Although one could say that protection of the privacy of human beings should be mandatory, sports organizations seldom acted according to this moral principle. Too many girls were betrayed by the one organization that should have remained silent. That should have protected their athletes. One of the victims was the Polish and Olympian gold medalist Ewa Klobukowska. She was tested twice. First, in Budapest, she took part in the aforementioned naked parade.[2] Although this "parade" was organized to unmask males and so-called hermaphrodites, Klobukowska passed the visual test. However, the IAAF remained doubtful of Klobukowska, and mistrusted the USSR. Being "suspect," it was planned that Klobukowska would be tested in Stuttgart. As West Germany fell outside the Eastern Bloc, the IAAF made use of the opportunity, and had her tested for a second time.

The European press paid a lot of attention to Klobukowska's gender test, which is not surprising, because their mistrust of the Eastern Bloc. The prejudices against athletes of the Soviet Union were then proven correct; the East had committed fraud, and the press made Klobukowska the scapegoat. The "real" women had to be protected against the "boyish" ladies of the Eastern Bloc.

At the same time, the Polish press remained completely silent regarding the affair in 1967. There was no news on the test, or the test result. Instead the Polish papers concentrated on doping matters in the West.[3] This probably was meant as a smokescreen.

Poland was part of the Soviet Bloc at that time, and there were serious geopolitical tensions between the West and the East at play. There were profound political and economic differences between the capitalist countries of the West and the USSR in the East. One could call it armed peace. The Cold War started after the Second World War, as Russia consolidated its control over the countries in the Eastern Bloc. These were the countries the Russians had liberated from Nazi Germany. With economic funds the U.S. supported the European countries they had liberated during the war. Although the U.S. and Russia had been allies, a great deal of mistrust between the two began growing two years after the end of the war. During the Cold War there were many military crises. This included the Berlin Blockade, the Korean War and the Hungarian Revolution in 1956.

Communist Russians had already left the Olympic movement in 1923. Competition and the winning of prizes were regarded as anti–Communistic. So Communist Russia and later the Soviet Union held its own sports competitions between 1923 and 1952.[4] Of course the competitors were just as eager to win as any other athletes.

The sports standard in Russia was high. We know this, in view of sports meetings between Russia and the Norwegian Socialist Workers Movement.[5] In Scandinavia, socialistic sports clubs organized their own speed skating competitions, outside the championships of the International Skating Union, ISU. The Scandinavian Workers also refused to participate in the International Skating Union and Olympic movement, just like the Russians. The skating championships of the Workers clubs were just as popular in Norway as in the Olympics or European skating championships. The Workers clubs were the only western clubs that competed against the Russians before the war. Skating was at that time the most popular sport in Norway.

Sometimes athletes deserted the Socialist clubs, such as Bernt Evensen, who won a gold medal in 1928 at the Olympics. Just before this event he was one of the Socialist speed skaters. So the workers were even more motivated to beat the capitalists, whether American or Norwegian. They were all the same. Although for the Socialists it was almost unforgivable to defect, Evensen still remains on the Olympic charts. All the others are lost and forgotten in the mists of social history. One weekend in Oslo, Norway, the International Skating Union held the European Championships and the

"They say I'm not a girl"

Socialists and Communists held their Workers Championship. Oslo had by that time two ice tracks: Bislett and Frogner, just a couple of hundred meters apart. During this memorable weekend it was Frogner against Bislett, capitalists against the socialists. That weekend the Russian Jakov Melnikov was the best speed skater in the world in three distances. Melnikov was also the world's best speed skater in 1928, the year of the Winter Olympics in Sankt Moritz. But there was no gold medal for him. He had no direct competitors from the west, but he still could race against the clock and beat their times. Melnikov is forgotten outside Russia. Being a Communist, he could not skate in the Winter Olympics of 1928.

But in fact, on both sides of the Iron Curtain, sports was the arena of a harsh competition, just as much between Socialist states as between capitalist states. It is still unclear who won the memorable match in Oslo, because each party had a different set of rules. But Russia and later the USSR remained very active on the sporting ground between 1923 and 1956. And in the 1930s medals were reintroduced into the Communist competition. Russian Avant Garde artists like Vavara Stepanova even designed beautiful constructivist sportswear. Sports was still deeply rooted in every layer of the Soviet society. In 1952 the USSR joined the IOC again. They were active in the games in Helsinki. But could they be trusted?

Russia joined the Olympic movement again probably because Joseph Stalin saw the opportunities of showing the world the strengths of the USSR. But the world did not trust the intentions of the Soviets. As we have seen, quite a few Soviet female athletes ended their careers once gender verification was performed on site. So, Western sports organizations were now convinced that the Soviets deliberately placed men into the female competition. They considered the Press sisters examples. As I have already mentioned, I don't believe in this. As regards sex and gender the Soviets were just as conservative as the West in the 1960s, and Russians still are.

In 1967 the Austrian Athletic Union was pretty embarrassed, as it turned out that their best female skier, Erika Schinegger, was in fact a man. The Austrian sports union was flabbergasted. They hardly understood intersex conditions. They wanted to cover up their problems as soon as possible, and not be compared to the Russians. Maybe "Erika" could quietly return to his home village, because the Russians might condemn Austria for committing gender fraud.

Poland, the homeland of Eva Klobukowska, had no doubts about her. And they still believe that the West tricked her into a medical examination as a form of revenge—as an act of war, it being the Cold War. But every country protects their suspended athletes. The Dutch are convinced Foekje Dillema was tricked. The South Africans call the suspension of Caster Semenya an act of racism. Therefore, it seems fair that the Poles protect their compatriot.

I'm personally convinced that Klobukowska was an intersex athlete. First of all, the final verdict was given by Russian and Hungarian doctors as opposed to ones from the West.[6] My second argument is that the chromosome test could easily have been replicated by independent institutions or genetic labs in Poland or the Soviet Union. Nobody refuted the scientific result with scientific arguments that Ewa (Eve) was a biologic and genetic female. And she is still alive today. So yes, she is intersex and was barred.

But if we compare the slender appearance of Klobukowska with that of the hypermuscular Czech Jarmila Kratochvilova—who still holds the record on the 800 meters, set in 1983—it seems very unfair that Ewa was suspended. Kratochvilova holds the longest standing athletic world record, but claims she never took banned substances.[7] Not even two-time gold winner Caster Semenya comes anywhere near this record. Specialists like Albert de la Chapelle are convinced Kratochvilova is hyperandrogenic,[8] just as Semenya is, but as a result of another medical cause. Kratochvilova might have a high T as a result of an adrenal disorder where adrenal glands produce high levels of testosterone (no need to go into details of the disorder[9]). So it's hard to accept that hyperandrogenic athletes are suspended when testosterone is produced by the testicles, and not banned when high levels of testosterone are produced by the adrenal glands. Both are testosterone producing glands. Kratochvilova, as well as Klobukowska, had a high T, but in this case one's a hero, the other sentenced for life. Which proves that gender verification is not about fairness, but about a subjective concept of gender.

The final verdict of the IAAF was that "Klobukowska had 'one chromosome too many to be declared female for the purpose of athletic competition.'"[10] I don't think the IAAF ever lied about the result of a gender verification. I know of no example. This does not mean that the federation had a moral right to suspend intersexual athletes. But I do think every intersex athlete in exile was indeed suffering from DSD, a woman with a disorder of sexual development.

The press reacted mostly negatively, and unfairly, really. *Time* magazine, for instance, wrote:

"They say I'm not a girl"

"There's nothing like a dame," sang the navy men in *South Pacific*. Not so, say physiologists. There are people who are something like a dame but are really men, or even a combination of male and female because nature has scrambled their chromosomes. Last week a star Polish athlete found "herself" in one of these anomalous categories and was barred on medical grounds from international competition.[11]

Scrambled chromosomes? Like scrambled eggs? Herself in quotation marks?

A cartoonist in Switzerland by the nickname of Tchutti gave a sexist reaction, meant to be hilarious at the time, about ugly, fat and lesbian female athletes. His conclusion was if you looked at several female athletes, without a doubt, all female athletes were biologically male. Tschutti ends with the question, "Is Ewa Klobukowska now finishing the military academy?"[12]

Newsweek had a headline: "Who Goes There? Ex-Miss or Missing X?"[13] A German popular magazine called *Blick* was clever enough with another play on words: "The Blond Eve Is Adam."[14] *Washington Post* on the same day: "Klobukowska Misses Test for Misses." It was the first time that the press would react to a suspension of an intersexual athlete. It went wrong in all sorts of ways, morally and factually. The reactions were made in bad taste; one extra chromosome does not necessarily mean that Eve is Adam. But what did editors know in the sixties? Maybe they were just glad that finally one athlete of the Eastern Bloc had been caught "cheating." They felt justified in making fun of a shy, introverted young woman, just 20 years old, who could not defend herself. But for the press it must have been proof that they had been right all along on USSR athletes, that the Press sisters were indeed the Press brothers.

The IAAF learned its lesson on the invasion of Klobukowska's privacy and stopped publicizing private medical information of an athlete. But the word was out: Klobukowska had a Y-chromosome. The test must have been a Barr Body Test. Klobukowska was missing a Barr Body in (part) of her cells, meaning she had some XY cells. An XY-cell has no deactivated X.[15]

According to urban legends Klobukowska mothered a son. *The Independent* reported: "Despite her masculine appearance, Klobukowska, who was born in Warsaw in 1946 (and had been raised a girl) was soon vindicated: in 1968, she became pregnant and successfully bore a son. It seems likely that she suffered a genetic abnormality, and was perhaps therefore

74

dealt an injustice by the testing regime of the day."[16] The writer seems not to have checked any sources for verification. Mothering a son when there's a Y in your genetic system is impossible. She did not have ovaries.

It's high time for Klobukowska's biography.[17] We haven't met Klobukowska in person yet. Ewa (Ewy) Janine Klobukowska was born on October 1, 1946, in Warsaw to a family of highly educated parents. Ewa is an intelligent, modest woman with an academic education. Before her retirement, she worked as an economist at Energomontaz Polnoc, a Polish company that makes industrial equipment. She is a highly respected Polish citizen. Although suspended from the elite sports competition, she was able to lead a reasonably normal life later in Poland. The Polish Olympic Committee strongly criticizes her suspension. They do not recognize it. The current Polish press is also still convinced that the suspension of Klobukowska is one of the biggest blunders in sports history and genetics. According to the Poles, Klobukowska was the victim of a superficial inspection and of the Cold War. The Poles still consider her disqualification as revenge from the West against the Soviet Union. The IAAF inspections would have focused solely on athletes from the Eastern Bloc. The fact that she was judged in the West probably led to suspicions in the Eastern countries.

Klobukowska has even been inspected twice by the IAAF. The federation approved her participation in the female competition in September 1966 in Budapest. The following year, for the European Cup in Kiev, the international federation again subjected her to further investigation. The German doctor Max Danz, head of the German Athletics Federation, strongly insisted on an inspection. This occurred, during one of the preliminary track and field events in the German city of Wuppertal. The chromosome analysis was carried out in the former West Germany. Although the 20-year-old Ewa was still allowed to start in Wuppertal, strong pressure was placed on the Polish federation to take her out of the European Cup due to the results of the analysis. The Polish national federation refused and Klobukowska then applied for the European Championships in Kiev. The international federation made the results of the investigation public. She was suspended for life. The IAAF subsequently canceled her records at the Tokyo Olympic Games with retroactive effect. Klobukowska found her suspension "low and stupid."

Ewa Klobukowska was a good sprinter in her youth, although her technique in 1963 was still not up to par the year before the Olympiad in Japan. She was young, had lots to learn and was very shy. She ran the 100 meters in

"They say I'm not a girl"

12.3 seconds at the age of 17. That's fast for a girl of only 17. The press called her a proverbial "ugly duckling" that would soon "swim in the big water." There was only one girl in Poland that could beat her, and that was coincidentally her former classmate Irena Kirszenstein (now Szewinska). The Poles already spoke of the phenomenal duo K-K: Kirszenstein-Klobukowska. The Dutch had F&F, the Poles K&K.

K&K were both young in 1964 at the Olympic Games in Tokyo. Together these two young women joined the Polish 4×100 meters relay team. With these two youngsters the relay team was "unknown," they were outsiders. America, as the record holder, was theoretically certain to win the relay and take home the gold. Nobody imagined that the Polish team could win. But they did. (For the sake of completeness, the team consisted of Ewa Klobukowska, Irena Kirszenstein, Teresa Cieply, and Halina Górecka.)

The Games almost passed over Klobukowska as in the spring she had torn one of her metatarsals after falling on the track. But she wasn't going to give up that easily, and continued training on her bike. By the time of the Olympics she was fit again and in top form. The 17-year-old Klobukowska won the bronze medal at the 100 meter sprint in 11.6 seconds and gold with the Polish team in the 4×100 relay in 43.6 seconds. Ewa was the last runner and closed a gap of three meters between the Poles and the Americans. After the victory, Ewa played a little game with the track staff, pretending not to hand over the baton to them. Her teammate Theresa Cieply quickly took over the baton from Klobukowska and took it to the locker room. Whether or not the baton has remained in Polish hands remains a mystery.

In 1965 on July 9, in Prague, Klobukowska ran a new world record in the sprint, where K&K would be starting side by side. But it started to rain and before the rain stopped it was dark and cold. The competition management wanted to cancel the competition, but as a formality, and, as the public was still waiting for the fireworks, the ladies were allowed to run later in the evening. Klobukowska and Kirszenstein both finished with the same time of 11.1. After a long examination of the finish photo Klobukowska was declared holder of the new record. The fireworks could begin. Back in Poland they both walked through an honorary hedge of their fans. Statisticians know that after Klobukowska's suspension, the world record passed onto her friend Irena Kirzenstein. There is no known documentation of her reaction.

The records have been erased of 100 meter and of the Olympic relay in Tokyo. Also, after the gender verification three years later, the relay world record was erased by the IAAF statistics in 1968. According to the *New York Times*, "The International Amateur Athletic Federation withdrew today ratification of all victories, medals and records achieved by Eva Klobukowska, the blond Polish sprinter who failed a sex test last year."[18]

The IOC did not officially react to the suspension, so the Polish relay team kept their Olympic title. They kept the gold. With these decisions by the IAAF and the IOC, we as spectators have a remarkable fact at hand: the American relay team won a silver medal in a new world record time of 43.9 seconds. To my knowledge this is the only time in sports history that a team lost a race in a world record time.

Just like the Dillema case, the records can be reinstated, as Klobukowska didn't benefit from elevated androgynous levels in the 100 meters. But different times, different mores. Klobukowska was suspended for having a male sex chromosome, and not for the benefits she might have had from this chromosome.

I'm not sure why Klobukowska remained under suspicion in 1967. Yes, she was extremely fast for a young girl, but so was Kirszenstein. There was no reason to test just Klobukowska because of her outstanding performance. Was it her boyish appearance? Looks don't count of course, but it was, after all, 1967. She was no biologic male nor a Klinefelter XXY. We can speculate on her genetic makeup; the best choice would be XX/XY. One correct set of chromosomes XX, the other set XY. XX and XY are the most stable cells. She was a mosaic for sure. But there are other possibilities. However, this speculation is not very relevant. After the Barr Body Test, further tests followed. A karyotype of her cells was undertaken, meaning a visual appearance of the chromosomes in her cells, by which the chromosomes are able to be identified and counted.

The Polish Federation refused to suspend her from national competition; she could still run. But the word was out. Klobukowska had the right to privacy, and the physicians had to respect that right, even in the sixties. The *Frankfurter Allgemeine*—one of Europe's leading newspapers—reported that Klobukowska underwent gonadectomy: undescended testicles had previously been removed from her abdomen.[19] This made it possible for her to get back in the competition. Such an intervention was obvious for intersexual athletes. Testicles produce testosterone, so after such an operation the T-value in the blood decreases considerably. Some of the masculine characteristics will slowly disappear. After the gonadectomy Klobukowska could no longer benefit from the high T (If there ever was an advantage for female athletes), but a T-level was not taken into consideration by the IAAF. These were the XX-Games. Chromosomes decided whether an athlete could return in the female competition. The Y-chromosome in part of her cells—still remaining—was decisive. The gender was defined by chromosomes—XX or you were out. Klobukowska wasn't the only woman tested twice.

The cause for Klobukowska's genetic makeup, was probably, as explained before, non-disjunction of the two copies of the X-chromosomes. It leaves one daughter cell with two X-chromosomes and a single copy of the Y-chromosome. XXY would be Klinefelter Syndrome. But they are males by definition. So just like in the Dillema case, there were many little failures in cell division, leaving her with a mosaic of cells with a different genetic make-up. Little mistakes with huge consequences if you want a gold medal, or want to have children.

Humiliated by the publicity, Klobukowska interrupted her studies and moved to Czechoslovakia. To this day, she still avoids the media when appearing in public meetings. She does, however, participate in social events and meetings of the National Polish Olympic Committee. They support her in every possible way. But she always keeps her distance from the press. Moreover, the Polish government presented her with the highest possible award known in Poland: the Golden Cross of Merit.

The Polish Olympic Committee still expresses objections in their sports biography of Ewa Klobukowska against the method of testing used by the IAAF in 1967. According to the committee, gender cannot be determined on the basis of a chromosome test alone. According to the POC it is a very uncertain way of determining gender, and the IAAF was seriously in the wrong because they did not consult the opinion of, for example, endocrinologists, professionals in the field of hormones. The committee therefore does not accept the suspension of Ewa Klobukowska and believes that she should be reinstated. According to the POC the gender verdict was not supported by other medical experts. The Poles stand by their champion.

Erika Schinegger

Gender Born or Gender Made?

Is being a boy or a girl a matter of genes through the father? Does a girl throw "like a girl" because she is a girl? Or is she made a girl? Is it, as the saying goes, "all in the genes," stupid? Or are hormones like testosterone the decisive factor in your gender? And can you raise a boy as a girl? Or vice versa? The Austrian skier Erik Schinegger was raised as a girl although he was biologically and genetically a man. And maybe, as a reaction to his upbringing as a girl, he grew into being a real macho man.

Raising Erik Schinegger as a girl was no experiment, of course. Although gender is fluid, there wouldn't be much enthusiasm for your actions if you chose to raise your baby boy as a girl. Still, it happens now and then, and sometimes on purpose because parents would have preferred a girl instead of having a boy! In other cases boys were raised as girls due to ambiguous genitalia. In these cases surgeons tried to correct the gender by operating at a very early age. And because it was easier "to dig a hole" than "build a pole,"[1] surgeons preferred digging a hole. The idea behind this surgery was that you could raise boys as girls and girls as boys. Don't try this at home. Many intersex adolescents became frustrated that they were unable to make their own decisions. Instead an irreversible decision was made for them.

Nowadays doctors wait until the child is able to make their own decision. It wasn't until 2001 that British surgeons argued for deferring vaginoplasty until adulthood on grounds of poor outcomes for women who were operated on as infants.[2]

A famous boy-raised-as-a-girl case is David Peter Reimer (who was not an athlete). Reimer wrote a book on being raised as a girl, and eventually—maybe as a result of his ruined youth—committed suicide. Wikipedia says:

"They say I'm not a girl"

David Peter Reimer (1965–2004) was a Canadian man born male but reassigned to being a girl and raised female, following medical advice and intervention, after his penis was accidentally destroyed during a botched circumcision during infancy.

Psychologist John Money oversaw the case and reported the reassignment as successful and as evidence that gender identity is primarily learned. But sexologist Milton Diamond later reported that Reimer's realization he was not a girl, crystallized between the ages of 9 and 11 and he transitioned to living as a male at the age of 15. Well known in medical circles for years anonymously as the "John/Joan" case, Reimer later went public with his story to help discourage similar pedagogic practices. He committed suicide after suffering years of severe depression, financial instability, and a troubled marriage.[3]

Trying to raise a child gender neutral—a recent trend in Scandinavia—is very difficult, if not impossible. Not only is the child capable of resisting its upbringing, but parents can send gendered signals to the child without meaning to. Such as keeping girls closer to the parent than boys, allowing less freedom to girls. Moreover, peer pressure influences the child to a large degree as well. Children spend a lot of time with their peers during most of their developing years. Parental influence, therefore, seems to be overestimated.

To raise a child without gender, the world around the child needs to change; having only gender neutral clothes and toys doesn't cut it. The child will watch Disney fairytales, and see old movies with specific gender roles. One cannot create one's own kind of child in a society that is based on gender. One would have to keep one's child away from competitive sports, as girls would be at a disadvantage. Mixed teams? How could one mix a soccer team, a rugby team or an ice hockey team when children are older? Injuries in the field would occur regularly in the case of mixed gender games. An ideal far from reality. Besides, would we choose to live in a gender-neutral world?

Back to the topic of this book: Are gender neutral sports competitions impossible? Surely girls would not be permitted to play on the same teams as boys. Most women would not be able to compete at a high level in a gender-neutral competition.

For example, power distance in track and field: the 800 meters. This distance is called a prolonged sprint, where power and endurance are required. Even the most powerful women, like Caster Semenya, are beaten by more than ten seconds by the best male runners. This is a gap of about 70 meters. The best male pitchers throw a baseball at the speed of 100 miles per hour: the record for women is 70 mph. Yes, girls can learn to throw a ball like a boy, with the same techniques and accuracy, but never with the same speed. The differences are quite obvious: there would be no place for girls in a gender-neutral competition. There is no fair place for women in male competition. Even the not-so-very-talented high jumper Dora Ratjen set the world record for females in 1939.

So everybody agrees with the necessity of separate male and female elite competition. The problem is, however, as already shown, nature doesn't always separate human beings clearly into men and women.

In the history of modern sports two biological males participated in elite female competition. They participated because they were raised as girls. It was a logical step for them. Dora Ratjen was one of them and Erika Schinegger the other. Both agreed with their disqualifications. But you cannot just wipe out the most important part of your life by declaring that from now on you will continue your life as a man. Heinrich (Dora) Ratjen refused to speak ever again about his youth as a girl and female elite athlete. Participation in the Olympic Games for him was worse than losing. Schinegger overcompensated when he started living his life as a man.

Until 2010—at least in the Western world—children with ambiguous genitals were raised as girls. The child had no choice. She was forced into a gender role that sometimes did not fit. But what could you do about it? Changing gender was not just a matter of a new wardrobe. It wasn't just telling your family and friends that you want to continue your life as a boy or man. They would probably stare at you in shock. Isolation and loneliness would follow. We know from case studies in the 1930s that some men lived happily ever after, but I tend to believe that most intersex people continued their lives as women after they were diagnosed. Maybe never knowing what made them so different from others was the reason for uneasiness and depression. Sometimes parents would feel uneasy and doubt the choice they made regarding the gender of their child. This uneasiness derives from nature itself.

Living in rural areas, people knew that in livestock the gender of a cow, a goat, a horse or a pig could be ambiguous. Cows could be freemartins due to excessive levels of testosterone of their twin bull. In a twin cow and bull, the cow receives the same amount of testosterone via the blood between them in the mother's uterus. This changes the cow's appearance and behavior. In dehorned goats, 30 percent of the nannies are intersexual. This is called the horn factor. Nowadays, in breeding goats, one of the parents must have horns. Otherwise there would be an explosion of hermaphrodite goats. These goats are infertile and destined for the butcher's block. Somehow the horns influence the gender of the offspring. Some mares behave as stallions due to the presence of testes in their abdomens. The same goes for some male pigs. Undescended testicles can also be a human condition, both in women and men. It is speculated that Adolf Hitler had one undescended testicle. Naturally there was gossip about babies with ambiguous genitals. People knew about the "abnormal" cases in livestock and heard stories of babies born "hermaphrodite." The midwives had sometimes seen the cases with their own eyes. Maybe that was why the mother of skier Erika Schinegger had her doubts about the sex of her child Erika. She lived on a farm in a small village in Austria.

The story of Erika is well known, because of the informative documentary *Erik(a)* made by Kurt Mayer in 2005.[4] This biography is mainly based on that film, and the quotations in the rest of this chapter, if not otherwise attributed, are from the film.

As a small child in Austria, Erika Schinegger did not like the dolls her mother gave her as Christmas presents. And her poor mother had done her best to sew and knit clothes for Erica's dolls. Erika didn't want dolls. Her eyes were glued to the shop windows in the city, windows that were full of cars, airplanes, trucks and tractors. Toys for boys. She wanted a tractor so much but got a doll again at Christmas. Angrily, she hit the doll's china head against the wall so hard that the skull broke. She got her tractor two days later. Most boys are born and not made.

Erik Schinegger was born on June 19, 1948, as Erika, on a mixed farm in Agsdorf, Austria. "My parents were close relatives, first cousins," says Schinegger in the film *Erik(a)*. Erik's father was past the age of 40 when a full cousin came to help him on the farm. They married, but according to Erik it was a marriage of convenience. Farmers do not have time for romance. They work from sunrise to sunset every single day.

These so-called cousin marriages are widespread, but can result in genetic disorders in their offspring. Marriages between cousins were legal in Austria but forbidden in most European countries at that time. In modern times in Europe these marriages are legal, but they are not fully accepted and sometimes seen as a medical risk for the children. These risks are overestimated. First cousin marriages are regarded with contempt in modern Western society. People tend to attribute diseases of the children born from these marriages to the familial relation of the parents. That is certainly not always the case and you have to take into consideration that many people in the West are descended from cousin marriages, because the first people that arrived from Africa into Europe were very small in number. So men and women found partners within these small populations, often a cousin in the first line. Marriages between cousins could even have been an effective cure for diseases like malaria.[5] So there is probably no connection between the cousin marriage of his parents and Erik's initial intersexual condition.

Erika was born on a farm in the small village of Agsdorf, barely visible on the map of Austria, near Villach and Klagenfurt. There are only six streets, one of which has been recently renamed the Erik Schineggerweg. It seems like all intersexual athletes were born in small villages: Burum, Wierzchonia, Polokwane, Kathakkurichi, Agsdorf ... this can hardly be a coincidence. Maintaining the social order is an important characteristic of society, even the smallest ones. An intersexual child is so far out of the standard order, that keeping quiet is always the best thing to do, to avoid the shame associated with extraordinary difference. An intersexual child is also out of the religious order, where God created male and female and nothing in between. One couldn't be both or none. There's no place in a village church where men sit on the one side and women on the other. There's no intersexual bench in church; no gender-neutral pew. Society is based on the dichotomy of male and female. You were either male or female. Life wasn't a cabaret of freak shows. If you couldn't adjust to the social norms, you had no choice other than to leave or continue your life behind closed doors and very lonely! If you were lucky you'd become the housekeeper of the local priest. Yes, I know it's a cliché, but that doesn't make it untrue.

Sexuality is unmentionable in these societies, which is another major aspect of hidden intersexuality. Primary amenorrhea, when a woman has never menstruated, can be a forbidden topic in rural families. I know this from my conversations with Aafke Dillema who told me that her sister's amenorrhea was not discussed in the family. Everybody knew, nobody spoke about it. It was the family's taboo.

A medical examination at an earlier stage could have prevented all the humiliation and suffering. The Dutch intersexual swimmer Carla de Vries was protected by the Dutch Swimming Union.[6] She stayed in the competition, but out of the spotlight. Erik Schinegger is a different story: he liked to be in the spotlight.

And yet Erik's condition could also have been noticed earlier. Namely when Erika was a toddler. It had already occurred to her mother that the skin was swollen in her groin. "The GP said it was a break, but that the child was too young to correct it. This didn't stop me from seeking further advice so I went for a consultancy and finally to the hospital in Villach. The doctors always said it would solve itself, but it has remained that way."

One of Erika's testicles later descended. Erika considered removing it herself: "When I was herding the cows, I got the idea to remove that ball myself. I had seen enough at home to see how they did it in the pigs. Such an intervention would not have been a good idea." To put it mildly! But it goes to show that Erika was struggling with her body, maybe even with her gender identity. But who was there to discuss it with her? Quite an embarrassment for a girl coming of age. And quite a burden too.

The children in Agsdorf regularly played with each other. They came together in the Schinegger orchard every Sunday after Mass. Hansi Naglreiter, who later became a baker, and the later "tüchtige hausfrau" Rosi Male, for example. In the summer they went swimming in the mountain lake and in winter skiing on the small hill near the Schinegger farm. They all look back on a happy childhood in the village. Erika was also happy as a child, although as we have seen that changed when puberty arrived. This was followed by a period of uncertainty, forcing her to play a game of hide and seek.

The somewhat simple village girl Rosi Male lived with her mother in the house of the Schinegger family. They took shelter in the Schinegger farm to get away from their aggressive father and husband. He was a woodcutter. (Sooner or later all fairy tales come true.) "We always lived in fear," Rosi says in the documentary. They had two rooms at Schinegger's large farm. Rosi and Erika took care of the small animals and often played in the hayloft. Rosi was the first person with whom Erika had a sexual experience. Erika, when she was thirteen years old, gave Rosi five shillings to see her naked. Five shillings was a lot of money for children at that time. Rosi saw no harm and undressed for her "girlfriend" Erika. Erik said at a later age: "It was important for me to see her naked. But I quickly turned around because I saw that it was wrong. Rosi then quickly got dressed again." And so Erika discovered the explanation for her uncertain existence: she was lesbian. "I found girls' bodies more beautiful, for an athletic boy I only had admiration. But I got excited about girls, but I also knew that it was forbidden. I also did not allow myself to be a lesbian. But I was no longer interested in boys. It ended when I was thirteen in a crisis and fled into the sport."

Erika did not have any periods. None. Erika lied and told the other girls that she had had her periods too. Erika did not develop breasts, so Rosi suggested that they buy a bra and pad it. Erika lived a life full of little lies.

His childhood friend Hansi Naglreiter remembered that in the summer, Erika went swimming with the other children less and less often: "Erika only went with us when it was dark. I felt like she wanted to hide something. Nobody spoke about it, but we knew something was wrong. Erika therefore became taboo for us boys." Erika became more muscular. It also showed in her face. For most people who knew Erika, this was self-explanatory. The family had a large farm and they worked hard. After all, there were other farm daughters who were boyish and strong.

In the winter the children evidently went skiing in the village. There were, however, hardly any official facilities in the 1950s. The children had to flatten the fresh snow themselves and climb up again every time after a descent. Erika was always the first on the mountain in the morning and did not leave until it was dark. Naglreiter remembered that she was often bossy; the others worked too slowly in her eyes. But her enthusiasm was contagious, and she managed to get the other children enthusiastic: "Her great commitment set an example for me. Other children complained that they were cold and that they were tired or that they had bad material. Erika was anything but mommy's darling. She always followed her own path and arranged everything herself."

Erika Schinegger had a natural talent for skiing. And not only because she was actually a strong boy. Even for a boy Schinegger was an excellent skier. He would prove that later as a man, too. Erika's first trainer, Hermann Goman, found her firm and masculine, but because farmer girls often worked hard, he never doubted her gender. Stephan Sodat, a downhill racer, remembered that "when we started sprinting or running long distance, she was always with the best guys." But she never showered together with the girls. Nobody cared. After all, farms never had a shower at that time. "I felt insecure without sportswear," Erik said, remembering his life as a girl.

Erika always dressed very feminine, even in dirndl, while most of the skiing women in those days wore trousers. Apparently, Erika felt that people would look upon her as a tomboy. She wanted to avoid that through wearing old-fashioned Austrian feminine clothes that she bought through the mail: "In the back of the catalog there were pictures with the sizes. I had size 48 with short legs."

At the age of 18 Erika was a member of Austria's national ski team that traveled to the world championships in Portillo, Chile, in August 1966. Girls of all nationalities lived there as friends among each other. They got to know all the competitors well at international competitions. They all stayed together in the same hotel. They became friends for life.

The winner of the silver medal of 1966, the Frenchwoman Mariëlle Goitschel, had conceived a naughty plan. With the help of her compatriot Annie Famose, they threw Erika out of her bed. "We then noticed that she had very muscular legs. They were not muscles of a woman," said Famose. In Portillo Erika Schinegger became world champion of the downhill. She defeated Mariëlle Goitschel, who won gold in the giant slalom at the 1964 Olympic Games in Innsbruck. Erika was only 18 years old. It is amusing to see on the film footage that Erika back in Austria is warmly kissed on the cheeks by all the men and that she is wearing a nice leather handbag. Thousands of people came to Agsdorf to celebrate this first Austrian victory with her. Thanks to the local municipality Erika received a piece of land that included a ski slope. Later, that piece of land tacitly came back into council hands. As a result of her new identity, Erika Schinegger was a star in 1966. The curtain would soon fall, though.

In order to get rid of cheaters and hermaphrodites from the Eastern Bloc (per Karl Heinz Klee, vice-chairman of the Austrian Olympic Committee), the IOC introduced a laboratory test for the 1968 Games. For most this was fine, but Western federations were afraid that they would be accused of sports fraud. The physicians of the Austrian Committee therefore decided to carry out this test themselves. The Austrian urologist Ernst Raas was involved: "In the autumn of 1967 the IOC informed us that a so-called sex control would be carried out. As responsible physicians, we have decided to use this generally applicable test itself. Some cells would be used from the cheek mucus to show the so-called Barr Body. The Barr Body shows that an athlete is female."

Ernst Raas said:

We were surprised in 1967 that without gynecological examination you could determine the sex of an athlete from the cheek saliva. Erika's upper body was not developed, but that was the case with more sportswomen. We often saw sports girls whose upper body was not in agreement with the lower body. Erika was not exceptional. Erika was a girl, the external genitals looked very feminine, even with small testicles in the big labia, it can remain undiscovered for a long time that a girl is actually a boy. Schinegger's genitals had grown inside, as it were, you could compare it with a glove inside the abdomen.

Erika Schinegger

The physicians of the Austrian Olympic Committee were naturally not happy with Erika Schinegger's test result: just one X-chromosome. No Barr Body. From further physical examination it became clear that Erika was a biological and genetic man. The committee subsequently was forced to remove Erika from the competition. Erika wouldn't ski in the Games of Grenoble in 1968.

The vice-chairman of the Austrian Olympic Committee, Karl Heinz Klee, admitted later that in 1967 he had hoped that Schinegger would withdraw from the sport and that he would henceforth continue his life as a man or woman quietly on his farm. That he would rather not officially register as a man. "The suspicion of fraud had to be removed as soon as possible. We were afraid that in addition to the Eastern bloc, Austria would also be accused of gender fraud." But Schinegger decided to "correct his gender" as he himself said. He was not a hermaphrodite, and he was not a transgender man either. He was a male from the start.

Erik corrected his gender development through four operations. He was 19 years old and underwent these procedures in complete isolation. It was January 1, 1968, and no one visited him in the hospital. He did not want that. Then he returned to his family home in Agsdorf. There he remained more or less in hiding for half a year. He also did not go to church where women and men were separated. At that point he would have had to choose. According to his mother, it took "half a year before he became human again." The press did not want to speak to him at all. The newspapers dodged him. They were hesitant to speak to him, let alone write about the situation.

Erik was a minor. His father had passed away and thus never knew that he had a son instead of a daughter. His mother was satisfied with the operation: "At last something is happening," she had thought. She said when Erik came out of the hospital, "Today she will come home and from now on we will call her Erik. I still said 'she.'" Erik was not a German name but his mother defended it, stating that in England many men are called Erik (the German version of the name is Erich). Erik came home, but he was no longer the big star of a year ago. There was no one to support him. He wore a brown suit and had his long dark locks cut short. In the summer when the tourists came Erik took his first steps on lover's lane. He avoided the village girls, but that summer, as he reported, he had sexual relations with at least four girls.

His friends in the ski world did not know what was going on. They were only aware that Erika would be operated on, but did not know why

one would operate on a perfectly healthy woman. Olga Pall, a former al-
pine skier from Austria, said, "I became pale when I heard that she would
be excluded. It was a big shock even though we had had such a great time
together." At the 1968 Winter Olympics of Grenoble Pall won the downhill
event. In addition to the Olympic gold, she had two World Cup victories
during her career, both in the downhill discipline. Erik decided to personally inform her of the operation after a few months had passed. He certainly
knew how to tell the news quickly. "He grinned at me and said: from now
on I am Erik." He had said it firmly to her. Pall was dismayed: "It was as if
Erika had died. I found it sad that Erika was no longer there. I could still
see Erika's traits in Erik, but could not see him as Erika anymore. Erika was
dead. We had to say goodbye to her." Pall was the only Austrian skier who
came near Erika's skiing times. Erik gave her all the medals she was entitled to. He did the same to Mariëlle Goitschel. Goitschel became world ski
champion with retroactive effect in 1966. Erik lost all the titles that he had
achieved as Erika. He had participated as a man in the women's competition, although he cannot be blamed for fraud. Of course, Erika had doubts
about her body and did not go to a doctor. She had told white lies about her
menstruation. But you have to bear in mind that Erika, just like Dora Ratjen, was only 18 years old and was socially, psychologically and physically
quite complex. There was no question of sports fraud, because there was no
intention in either case to cheat.

Erik bought *Der Knigge,* the German-language version of the classic
etiquette book by Emily Post. Erik wanted to learn to be a courteous man.
"Ein richtiger Kavalier," said Olga, "he now knew how to light up the cigarette of a woman." But Erik wanted more. He also wanted to prove that
he was a real man. His first wife Renate calls him a real macho man in
retrospect. "I thought he would understand women well because he had
lived as a girl for 18 years, but the opposite was true." He behaved in a very
manly way: "It was overcompensation." Schinegger drove his new Porsche
to his old friend Naglreiter who was afraid that a man was suddenly standing in front of him. They had to go swimming, announced Erik. He had
put his swimsuit next to him in the car and just undressed outside, along
the waterfront. "He was proud that he was better built as a man than all
his friends."

Erik still wanted more. He wanted to prove that he was an excellent
skier as a man. So he went to the Austrian ski championships at his own ex-
pense. He participated after the first sixty skiers who had received an invi-

tation. Those were the places for the athletes or fans who wanted to gamble on getting a place. The journalist Wolfgang Winheim remembered that he was leaving after the sixtieth descendent, too scared to have to write about Schinegger. Schinegger had a great day. He finished sixth despite his late start time, good for a place on the national team. But he was not allowed. The Austrian ski association decided that Schinegger could not be included in the national team due to the unrest and the fuss it would cause. Erik had to learn that he was no one special again. Others had decided that for him.

Erik became even more macho than he already was. The real proof for his manhood came when he fathered a daughter, Claire. He was proud of his "achievement" and everyone had to know. Later he stated: "I used my daughter to prove that I was a man," he admitted, to his disgrace. "I finally had an argument that no one could disprove." But people are always inventive and naturally wondered if it was all a fraud and who this stand-in daughter was. However, Claire is Eric's biological daughter. There is no doubt about that. She has long lived with the idea that while her father's virility does not concern her, she served as proof of her father's masculinity.

To earn a living, Erik started a ski school for children aged 4 to 9. It was the only ski school that gave guarantees, so-called *Erfolgsgarantie*. As I write this book, the ski school is still very active and popular in Austria. Schinegger has taught thousands of children from all over Europe. He remarried and became a grandfather. At a later age we see Erik in the documentary about his life as a calm, confident, but modest family man.

Mariëlle Goitschel has the last word on Erika: "It was a double act, but I was always on her side. Athletes are always victims of the system. They benefit from the system but they are also victims of it. I defend her. You can condemn the doctor and the Austrian ski association. Even though I love Austria a lot. The friendships among the ski ladies have not suffered from this affair."

Stella Walsh

The Murder of the Polish Flyer

Stella Walsh was killed in the late afternoon of December 4, 1980. The former gold medalist of the 1932 Games had had a few drinks before she went to Uncle Bill's to buy ribbons to greet a delegate of Polish visitors in Cleveland. Maybe the brandy made her reckless. She tried to seize the .39 that was aimed at her, but then the gun went off and a bullet hit her in the stomach and ripped open a blood vessel in her pelvis. Two robbers were out for her money. Needless to say, in this type of situation the best advice is to give the money and save your life. After the gunshot, the robbers panicked and got away; a local police officer found Walsh unconscious by her car. Although her wig had fallen from her head, the officer recognized her. The ambulance, on its way to the scene of the crime, got a flat tire, so the officer brought Walsh in his car to the hospital. She died on the operating table. She wore her golden Olympic ring; her bra was filled with rubber foam.[1]

In 2016 Rob Tannenbaum wrote an excellent long read on Walsh called "The Life and Murder of Stella Walsh" (available at longreads.com). There's no need to do his research all over again so I quote from the article in this chapter. Matt Tullis wrote an interesting short biography in 2013: "Who Was Stella Walsh?"[2] Even using these two excellent sources I did double-check the coroner's conclusions to get the precise information on her genetic makeup and phenotype. I also read the biography of Helen Stephens on her relationship with Stella Walsh.[3]

Walsh wasn't the only murder victim that week. Four days later, news of the death of the former sprint star was overshadowed by the murder of John Lennon. He was also transported in a police car to the hospital. The officer asked him if he was John Lennon. He moaned a simple "yeah" and died in the police car. Lennon's death shocked the entire world; the death of

Stella Walsh

Stella Walsh, the winner of the gold and later silver medal, was just a minor affair compared to the death of the former Beatle. Still, there was a shocking revelation the evening before Walsh was buried. Someone from the coroner's office leaked to the press that Stella Walsh wasn't a woman. The news station WEWS in Cleveland broadcast the news: "Coming up next: Was Stella a fella?"[4]

Stella Walsh was 69 years old the day she was killed. She worked for Cleveland municipal recreation department, a job she had received out of charity from Mayor Dennis Kucinich. She gave sports lessons to the junior Olympic team of the city. Walsh had been to a café in the afternoon of December 4, 1980, and later had visited her bedridden 84-year-old mother, Veronica. Walsh lived in the Polish district of the city of Cleveland, Ohio.

She was born as Stanislawa Walasiewics—nicknamed Stasia—on April 11, 1911, in the Polish village Wierzchownia in the middle of Poland. When she was one and a half years old, the family emigrated to the U.S. Her father found a job in a steel factory in Cleveland, which was a city with a large Polish community. In the 1930s, there were 36,000 Poles living there. When Walsh died, the Polish community numbered 9,000. Walsh would remain loyal to this community throughout her life. She became an American citizen when she was 36, after the war, in 1947.

Although she had been in the spotlight for almost thirty years, she lived a reclusive life in the years before her death. Because she had achieved her great sporting achievements as a Pole, she never received a major American tribute. She had, however, had become a local celebrity by 1980 in her hometown. The press at large paid little attention to her in the 25 years before her death. And if she had not been killed, we would never have known that she had a particular genetic makeup. She would have gone down in history as one of the most important sprinters of this century. Now, doubt was introduced.

Walsh was a multi-talented athlete, as was Fanny Blankers-Koen, who came later. Walsh, however, won "only" one Olympic gold medal. That was at the 100 meters at the Los Angeles Games.[5] Furthermore, she won a silver medal in Berlin and two golds and two silver medals at the European Athletic Championships. As a 17-year-old she was already at the top. In 1928 she earned a place on the American Olympic team, but because she was not yet able to apply for American nationality at that age, she was not allowed to go to Amsterdam. She would have been able to excel in the Netherlands despite her youth. In her sports career she won 41 titles, and she improved

20 world records in various disciplines: discus and javelin, long jump, golf, medium distances and of course her specialty, the sprint.

After her sports career, things went downhill for Stella. In three decades she had asked too much of her body. When her father died, she moved to her mother's small apartment. She started drinking. She went to the liquor store three times a week where she bought liqueur and brandy. On the autopsy table the coroner found that she had ruined her liver. Her heart was weakened by high blood pressure. According to the coroner she would have lived for a maximum of another three years. It is a meager consolation.

"One of the great women of sport was murdered last night," Walter Cronkite reported on the *CBS Evening News*. "Stella Walsh, who was 69, was shot and killed in a Cleveland parking lot. No suspects have been arrested." The Polish community in Cleveland, but also in Poland, was shocked. Some Americans too, even though they did not always keep her in their hearts.

Whenever a person gets killed, there is an autopsy. And on the eve of the funeral a policeman leaked to Tom Beres, from the local television station WKYC, the sensational story that Walsh was not a woman, but a man. According to Beres, the source said that "Walsh had male genitalia." The news was widely reported. Beres made the news known on television that night: "Stella Walsh had a penis." The WEWS news station headlined the following day: "Stella Was a Fella." It could hardly be more vulgar. The 400 people attending her funeral were furious. The timing of the news could not be more disastrous. They threatened to sue the news channel for slander. The WEWS telephone was red-hot the next day.

Cleveland was even more shocked, Poland was outraged, but also many outside the Polish community were surprised by this hard news fact, which of course was not entirely correct. Undoubtedly there were also people who were not surprised to have their suspicions proved correct. As was common in those years, there was a lot of gossip in the sports circuit and beyond. But nobody knew for sure. Neither did the coroner. Walsh was buried under a simple stone with her Polish name, the Olympic rings and the text "Olympic Champion" in capital letters.

Walsh broke a record as often as she ran; in 1930 she set three new records in one tournament. That was in Philadelphia and she could have run the 220 yards even faster if she had not looked back playfully to see where the rest of the field was. According to the *New York Times* it was "one of the most starting performances that a woman athlete ever has fashioned." Of course, this newspaper hoped for her participation in the 1932

Olympics. At her temporary residence in Europe that year, the French newspaper *L'Equipe* wrote that it was "sad that she had to shave every day."

Even great sportswomen rarely escape judgment about their physical beauty, which transcends their athletic qualities. That is still the case, but in the 1930s when women's athletics were on the rise, appearance was discussed mainly negatively. It was said that female athletes had beards and Adam's apples, were lesbian, aggressive and wore false nipples where other women had breasts and moreover, most of them had taken a sex test to determine if they were really women. According to *Time*, Walsh "had a grey face, a Slavic look in her eyes, was broad-shouldered and muscular." Athletes rarely stood the beauty test. Moreover, according to many, women's running was like "a snail creeping through a salt layer."

Women who did pass the beauty test, like the swimmer Eleanor Holm, were in the first place beautiful and in second place great sportswomen. This held true as long as she was a fast swimmer or sprinter. Everything is relative: Johnny Weissmuller held the Olympic record on the 100 meters freestyle at 58.6 seconds. Today the world record for women is 51.7. Weissmuller is regarded as one of the best swimmers in history, but the fact is that by today's standards he was really not very good.

In 1930 Walsh visited Europe for the World Games in Prague. She won the 60, the 100 and the 200 meters. The tournament management overloaded her with gifts. And of course she also visited Warsaw in that period. The Poles wanted to "keep" her and offer her a well-paid job. But the 19-year-old Stasia turned down the offer, because she wanted to go to the 1932 Los Angeles Games as an American.

The year of the Olympic Games in Los Angeles, 1932, was a chaotic year for Walsh. She was 21, grown up and held promise for the Games in the only homeland she had ever known, America. She had equaled the world record of the Frisian Tollien Schuurman at 100 meters: 11.9. The battle in Los Angeles would therefore be between the Netherlands and the United States. But Poland took the gold.

In the Olympic year of 1932, Walsh worked for the New York Central Railroad Office, which used her sprinting fame as an advertising medium for the modern, fast 5200 Hudson locomotives: on old advertising photographs we can see Walsh running in front of such a locomotive.

Officially, however, she had an office job in cargo handling. But her department was closed two weeks before the start of selection games for the Olympics. Her father had only part-time work and had five mouths to feed.

Walsh decided to surprise the Americans with naturalization. She was able to work as a civil servant in Cleveland's recreation department. She would run for the United States at the 1932 Olympics in Los Angeles.

But the American Athletics Union (AAU) stopped her. Walsh received a telegram from the AAU stating that "when an athlete had a sports-related profession, the amateur status was canceled." Without that status she could not play sports because athletics was almost exclusively practiced by amateurs in those days. Walsh took the telegram with her the evening of her naturalization, to let them know why she was renouncing American citizenship. Her coach begged her to continue the naturalization. In vain. Therefore, she would run for Poland at the Los Angeles Games. The Poles were naturally pleased by this news. Stella had become Stasia again. The Polish government gave her a job at the Polish consulate in New York and the press laughed scornfully that it was a hidden subsidy. It was, of course. She lived too far from New York, but the athletics associations agreed to let her run; they could not argue with it. Walsh formally adhered to the rules.

The Americans decided they had had enough of Walsh in 1932. The newspapers even thought that she had to be removed from the competition because she did not run for any country. She ran "completely for herself." Moreover, her subsidized fake job was disguised professional sports play. Columnists called on the IOC to suspend her, because her semiprofessional status would be the virtual end of the Olympic Games. We can hardly imagine this nowadays, but at that time hardly anyone supported professional athletes at the Olympiads. The Games had to be free from something as banal as money. Making money as an athlete was immoral. The hidden agenda of this principle had once been to exclude the workman from sports activities. Sport was an activity of the bourgeoisie. Anyway, besides the Games, there was of course an extensive professional competition in all kinds of sports and the competitions were well attended. Often there were traveling sports circuses in the United States that held a "world championship" in every city they visited.

Walsh herself, who had little choice, shrugged her shoulders: "I am Polish, I am running for Poland," she said. What else could she do? But deep in her heart she preferred to compete for the U.S. Poland was her second choice. She now became an outsider in her homeland. It was not easy; she slept with her spikes under her pillow, afraid they would be stolen. It did not get much better when she broke the skull of a spectator with her discus.

She was arrested for deliberate assault but ultimately, of course, she was acquitted. She could not help it. There was no intention at all to hit anyone. It was an unfortunate accident.

The two main American competitors of Walsh—Eleanor Egg and Betty Robinson—both got injured before the Games. The 16-year-old Robinson barely survived a plane crash. She would never be able to run again. It wouldn't be American sprinters in this "American" Olympic year to win the medals. That was certain beforehand.

At the Games of Los Angeles, Stella Walsh won gold for Poland on a warm Sunday afternoon before 50,000 spectators. She wore a dark beret on her head. Second was the small Canadian Hilda Strike and third the very tall sprinter with the all–American name Wilhelmina Von Bremen. Hilda Strike finished very close as second and was awarded the same time as Walsh: 11.9. This equaled the world record of Tollien Schuurman. Schuurman was in Los Angeles and was the most important competitor, but she was left on her own after the Dutch Athletic Union dismissed her coach, Jan Britstra, who was her support and refuge. Schuurman still ran a good first heat, but then became uncertain due to a false start. She finished fourth in the semi-finals. That was a disappointment, because Schuurman was the first woman to have clocked within 12 seconds at 100 meters. That was on June 5, 1932, in Haarlem, the Netherlands.

The Poles were obviously proud of their Olympic champion and Stella decided to return to her homeland where she was welcomed back as a hero. She received the Golden Cross for Merit, the highest Polish award. Stasia participated that season in the major European tournaments and ran a new world record in Poznan at 100 meters: 11.8 seconds.

Stasia met Tollien Schuurman again in Schaarbeek, Belgium.[6] Schuurman beat her on both 100 and 200 meters, getting her revenge. Schuurman finished the 200 meters in 24.6, half a second above the world record of Walsh. Later it turned out that Walsh had run her 200-meter record on a straight track. It was not until the 1980s that the IAAF corrected her time and Schuurman regained the world record retroactively. However, Schuurman would not be a threat to Stasia at the upcoming Games in Berlin. Schuurman refused, as she said, "to run for Hitler and his henchmen" and stayed at home, in Friesland, the Netherlands.

Schuurman has been forgotten mainly because she never won a big tournament. The Dutch Athletic Union suspended her for life in 1936 because she refused to go to Berlin. Sports and politics had to remain separate, according to the chairman of the Union Ad Strengholt, who had personally gone to the village Rottevalle in Friesland to persuade Tollien. But Tollien, who grew up in a social democratic family, couldn't be convinced. Even though it was her last chance to win the gold, she stayed home. Walsh was now the designated winner for the Games in Berlin. The gold was already reserved for her, as they say. But Berlin would become a deception for Stasia and Poland.

For there was the American Helen Stephens, a sturdy, blond six-foot-tall athlete. Her nickname was "The Fulton Flash," after her native town, Fulton, Missouri. Stephens was a tough farmer's daughter who ran a mile to school every day in her youth. Her school friend rode on her horse and Stephens jogged along. Her classmates nicknamed her Popeye. She had a low voice because a wood splint got lodged in her larynx when she was a child, and she had remarkably big feet. She was a tomboy and full of life despite the fact that she had been raped at the age of nine by a 16-year-old boy, a relative, as she recounted in the memoirs that appeared after her death. Stephens was discovered as an athlete at a school competition. She was 15 years old when her coach, Burton Moore, clocked her at 5.8 seconds in the 50 yards; 5.8 was equal to the world record. It was her first official match. Moore then went to a jeweler to have his stopwatch checked. The watch was correct. Moore had discovered a major talent and decided to train her for sprinting distances. The coach kept this secret for a time. Two years later she experienced her first highlight at an indoor championship in St. Louis. It was to be the first confrontation between Helen Stephens and Stella Walsh, who had returned to the U.S.

The stands were packed, because everyone wanted to see Stella Walsh, the fastest woman in the world. But Stephens easily beat the Stella Walsh-phenomenon at the 50-yard final. Walsh, who could not stand losing, said that Stephens had made a false start. Moreover, she had the excuse that she had eaten badly and slept badly. She was not, however, usually someone who worried about anything and everything; the night before a match she always slept like a baby, not hindered by tension. She was not bothered by what she called the "feminine temperament." In short, she had simply lost. No excuses. A faster lady had appeared on the battle scene, at least on the short distance, where the start is the most important aspect of the race.

The press asked Stephens if she was proud of defeating Stella Walsh. "Stella who?" she answered. She was fooling around. The story goes that Stephens had a photo of Walsh above her bed and stuck a new pushpin in it every day. This is probably not true. But in the newspapers they openly mocked each other. Stephens was a beanstalk, according to Walsh, and Stephens said she would beat Walsh in her bare feet. The arguments got so heated that Walsh was expelled from her association for insulting an opponent. Walsh, who was always full of self-confidence, now had to recognize Stephens as a tough opponent. Although not much later, Walsh ran a world record again on the 70 yards and in the 200 meters, a record that lasted 17 years. But Stephens was there to stay. Stephens was not only good at track events. She played basketball, fenced and swam. Her biggest achievements, however, were the 100 and 200 meters running. Women were not allowed to participate in more than three Olympic competitions in 1936. So Stephens qualified for the sprint, the relay race and the discus. But with the discus she was short by meters in Berlin.

Berlin, 1936. This was also known as the Nazi Games. Hitler's propaganda machine. The 100 meters for women in Berlin was watched by 100,000 spectators. They saw that, although Walsh ran the world record, she was easily defeated by the tall, blonde American with the big feet. Stephens was then just 18 years old. She ran a time of 11.4 seconds in the first heat. This time was not accepted as a world record because of the strong back wind. In the final she ran 11.5, a new world record. That record would last for 24 years, until 1960. Stephens also took the gold in the relay race with her team, because the strong German team was disqualified for losing the baton. The American sports press selected Stephens as athlete of the year for 1936.

Stephens was called to the Führer's box. Hitler brought the Hitler salute. Stephens answered, in her own words, with "a good old-fashioned Missouri handshake." Hitler, who was impressed by her height, blonde hair and blue eyes, suggested she should run for Germany in the future. He invited her for a weekend at his country house at the Berghof. Stephens thought that Hitler's autograph was more than sufficient. She collected autographs. A photograph of the meeting between Stephens and Hitler in the Olympic Stadium was distributed in Germany as a postcard.[7]

Then the gender chaos started. The Polish newspaper *Kurier Poranny* claimed that Helen Stephens was a man. Their Stasia would certainly have won in a field of only women. The German runner Marie Dollinger, who came in fourth, even claimed she was "the only woman in the race."[8] She also had doubts about her teammate Käthe Krauss, who had come in third. *Look* magazine made the chaos even worse with the straight question,

"They say I'm not a girl"

"Is this a man or a woman?" above a picture of Helen Stephens. Stephens was summoned to visit a gynecologist in Berlin. The final verdict was "woman." Stephens was a woman who had rightfully won the gold. The assumption that Stella Walsh was behind the accusation seems pretty unlikely to me. She knew, of course, that her gender was unclear. She kept quiet, congratulated Stephens and disappeared from the stage.

Stephens blossomed in Berlin, far from her strict Christian parents. She met Goering at his castle, who flirted with her in his dressing gown. He had no chance, as Stephens was having, as she said in her memoirs, a short-lived, torrid romance with the German waitress Ruth Haslie. Stephens' sex life is widely documented in the memoirs that were recorded by a college friend, Sharon Hanson. Of course, the book was only allowed to appear after Stephens' death. She had been very open about her sex life. She said, among other things, that she wanted a sex-changing operation after the Berlin Games. Stephens wanted to become a man. And to the amazement of many readers, Avery Brundage would have supported her in her wish. This operation was not carried out, as far as we know.

In her memoirs she also remembered that during a tournament in West Virginia she had a room next to Walsh and that Walsh had been heavily involved with two other women.[9] Stephens shared her room with her own girlfriend. An anonymous member of the Hall of Fame organization remembered the racket of drunken girls. Eventually they decided to give Walsh some money and put her on a bus to Cleveland. But neither Walsh nor Stephens came out of the closet during their lifetimes. That would not have been very sensible, given the spirit of the times and the prejudice that all sportswomen were lesbian. Moreover, Walsh distrusted almost everyone. Stephens was not popular with many men, either. Tossing a baseball from one hand to the other, she challenged men who obviously were not up to her.

After the Olympic Games, the competition started in Europe. Stephens won almost everything, but Walsh did beat her twice. Stephens, however, was forced to quit due to the economic situation at home. She had to earn money for her parents and thus became a professional basketball player in the U.S. She invited Walsh to also give up amateur status and to start running for money against her in the U.S. Walsh turned down the offer. She would quit, too, but returned to amateur competition after the war. Stephens was lucky because Jesse Owens also joined the professional competition. He was suspended for life by Avery Brundage because he refused to go on a post–Olympic tour in Europe. He was too tired, he needed rest after the Olympics. There was a lot of money to be earned in the U.S. Owens ran against Stephens, and she got a head start in every race. It was gold against gold, and the Americans wanted to see their champions. Jesse Owens started to give lectures too. And he had no complaints about popularity or income. Everyone wanted to hear the story of the man who had put Hitler in his place by defeating the German so-called "Ubermensch." By the way, Hitler was not impressed by Owens—as he said to Albert Speer: "Jungle people do not belong in the sports competition."

Stephens worked in a Navy airplane factory during the war. Like many American women, she contributed to the war effort. After the war she founded her own female basketball team called the Helen Stephens Olympic Co-Eds. She toured the U.S. for seven years with this team. She finally went to teach at her alma mater, William Woods College, as assistant sports coach. She died in January 1994 in Missouri. She had never been defeated at official competitions. She had two gold Olympic medals in her pocket. And led a memorable life. And yes, in 1980 she had also read the news about Stella Walsh.

Walsh continued as an amateur athlete after the war. She spent the war in the U.S. and in December 1947 she received U.S. citizenship. That, she said, "gave her the most satisfaction of her life." She had decided to win a golden Olympic medal for the USA out of gratitude. But she apparently had not read the rules: an athlete could not come from two different countries in her lifetime. Stella Walsh was denied the starting right by the American Athletics Union at almost every match. But eventually there's a solution for everything.

In 1956, the IOC amended their regulations. An athlete could from then on participate at the Games for a new county if he or she married a partner from the new country. Walsh then got married, to the boxer Neil (also called Harry) Olson. Walsh was 45 and Olson 33 when they flew to Las Vegas for a quick wedding. The marriage was short-lived and not exactly romantic. It must have been a difficult decision for Walsh, in view of her disturbed gender development. Olson said that they had only had sexual intercourse a few times and always with the lights off. They were also rarely together. He regretted the fact that he had even met Stella Walsh. He was bullied at work. He tried to get the marriage declared invalid, because according to him the marriage could not have been legal. "I feel stupid as hell, marrying her," he said in a newspaper. However, silence became ultimately the best option. He refused to talk about it further, despite the urging of the press and friends.

There was a legal separation between Olson and Walsh, but Walsh continued to use the name Olson for the rest of her life: Stasia Olson-Walasiewics. With her marriage she had her Olympic ticket back, but could not redeem it anymore. She was eliminated in 1956 in the preliminaries of Las Vegas two weeks after the wedding. But she was named the third best American athlete ever and thus she finally beat her rival Helen Stephens, who finished tenth.

Stella Olson-Walsh, meanwhile, started drinking. Her hair became thin and in another robbery a thief smashed her nose. She was 45 but, according to many, seemed to be 65. And of course the Polish children she trained in Cleveland also joked about her behind her back. She was caught several times with stolen items. In Longansport police officers found six fur coats in her car. She went to jail but was not convicted because the court refused to pay the travel expenses of the witnesses. No witnesses, no conviction. Walsh was released.

Walsh's post-war life was often a series of personal misfortunes mixed with sporting highlights. She continued to win the 100 and 200 sprint in the U.S. even into a reasonably advanced age. She sold her medals and ribbons and so on cheaply, for drinking money. When she was robbed and shot in Cleveland, she had twice the permitted alcohol level for driving in her blood. Was she an easy target because of the drink? Possibly.

It took several years before Walsh's killers were arrested. The investigation first focused on Nancy Jo Dale, a former lover of Walsh who had not attended the funeral. Dale was also a heavy drinker, but she was not in Cleveland on the night of the murder. One of the problems, however, was that she told a different story every time she was interrogated, so the police continued to suspect her. Dale eventually ended up in a psychiatric clinic.

In the meantime, $5,000 had been offered for a tip that led to the murderers. The golden tip came three years after the murder, from a prisoner. On the night of the murder he had heard the robbers at a party telling them that a robbery had gone wrong and that the weapon had suddenly gone off. In 1983 Donald Cassidy and, later, his brother-in-law Rickie Clark were arrested. The two criminals confessed, and received a reduction in their penalty to ensure that no further judicial investigation would be conducted on Stella Walsh. The judges wanted to put her posthumous suffering to an end. Rickie Clark was a born criminal who was imprisoned for much of his life. Cassidy, the man who had fired the shot, was a totally different type of criminal—he became the perfect prisoner. He converted to Islam in prison and studied social sciences there. While in prison he published a scientific article about psychological support for prisoners and its influence on recidivism. After his sentence was completed, he worked for various social organizations.

But the sensational news had been on the streets three years before the arrest, thanks to a talkative police officer. In December 1980 the public demanded from the coroner an explanation about the gender of Stella Walsh. People demanded to know what was true about the rumor that Walsh was a man or "hermaphrodite."

Because the coroner, Samuel Gerber, did not have a complete answer to the question, he had ordered a chromosome analysis, although this was not necessarily for the trial.[10] This analysis was to answer the question of what the genetic gender of Walsh was. The chromosome analysis showed that she had two sets of sex chromosomes, XY and X0 (X-zero). There was a complete set of normal cells, XY, and an incomplete set of cells, X0[11]—body cells with only one sex chromosome, an X. But there were more X's than Y's. As we have seen before, this is a genetic mosaic. The clinical manifestations are variable, ranging from partial virilization and ambiguous genitalia at birth, to patients with completely male or completely female gonads. Most individuals with this karyotype have apparently normal male genitalia, and a minority present with female genitalia, with a significant number of individuals showing genital abnormalities or intersex characteristics. But Stella had been raised as a girl. Probably at birth her gender was ambiguous. Childhood friends later claimed that they had previously known that "she was a hermaphrodite." That she was "a mistake of nature." According to these friends, it was generally known in the neighborhood. Walsh's sisters were silent about her. They did not want to say anything about it.

Coroner Gerber insisted that Stella Walsh was a woman: "John Lennon," he said, "we knew as a man, he was murdered as a man, and the autopsy shows that he was a man. Stella's birth certificate says she is a woman, we knew her as a woman and her death certificate says she is a woman. Socially, culturally and legally we should therefore consider her as a woman." He hoped that this would put an end to the discussion, but this did not always prevent her from being known posthumously as "Stella the Fella." And he also could not prevent the newspapers from writing that Stella had been a man. And thus, a deceiver. Even now, that remains a problem.

The television station that remained under fire demanded that Gerber should release the autopsy report. Gerber refused until a judge forced him to do so. In the report, Gerber writes that Walsh had a small, undeveloped, non-functional penis with no opening for urine or semen. Walsh had no vagina or uterus and only a small opening through which to urinate. She had a scrotum with undeveloped testicles. She could therefore not menstruate and her breasts appeared male. Undeveloped testes produce no sperm, but can account for an elevated T-level.

According to most newspapers, she was a man. Gerber, however, confined himself to the facts in the autopsy report and avoided the personal pronouns he and she. He left the final verdict about her gender to his colleague Dr. Lester Adelson, who explained that "the gender of Walsh was not black or white. She was neither male nor female. Nature does not always manifest itself clearly."

That she was hyperandrogenic leads little doubt. Her testosterone level must have been high for a woman. However, Stella Walsh did not have a really deep voice. You can listen to that yourself via YouTube because on September 6, 1954, she was a guest on the radio show *You Bet Your Life*, hosted by Groucho Marx. Stella was humorously clever. She was then 43 and still active at the top. She ran, as she tells Marx, against girls who were not even born when she was winning her first championship.

After her death in 1980, the IOC considered taking away her medals. After all, we were still in the period of sex tests and intersex athletes being taken out of competition. But for the time being, nothing happened. Yet the fire smoldered. For example, the Canadian Hilda Strike, who had come in second in Los Angeles and found Walsh very masculine, angled for a change of record. Strangely enough, Walsh continued sending Strike Christmas cards until her death—according to Strike, out of guilt. Strike's grandchildren lobbied the IOC to give their grandmother the gold medal. It was Helen Stephens who then stood up for Walsh: "Taking away her medals would be a cruel act. I do not think she was a man," she said. "I do not believe that Walsh benefited from her birth defect. It was not her fault anyway." Stephens was less positive about her former opponent later in her memoirs. "She had something extra," she wrote.

In 1991, the Athletic Congress decided that Walsh was allowed to keep her records and medals and offered excuses for the damage that had been done to her. However, Walsh's gold medal from Los Angeles is still missing. Without a doubt it was sold for a bottle of brandy.

Maria José Martinez Patiño
The First Protest

Former Dutch swimmer Carla de Vries told me in a personal interview that she was 54 years old before she first heard from a doctor that she was an intersex female. When she was a teenager, she had been examined extensively by a specialist because she did not have her periods. "It was something hormonal, the doctors told me. But there still remained a secret that I just couldn't figure out." As it turned out, this secret was known within the Dutch swimming union (KNZB). She said:

> At 54 I visited a gynecologist together with my husband. As I entered the room he said that he could see from my face that I was a fella. I had no idea what he was talking about. Apparently he had read my old medical dossier on the examination that was done 25 years ago. He couldn't believe I was married and my husband first had to get his passport and the marriage certificate before the doctor wanted to talk to us both. It was baffling, we hadn't the slightest idea what could be going on.

De Vries is a woman with XY chromosomes. Genetically she is male, but her core gender identity is female. In more scientific terms, her genotype doesn't fit her phenotype. According to her sex chromosomes she should have been born as a man. She was born a woman.

De Vries lives as a woman, was at birth assigned as a girl, was raised as a girl, married a man and looks completely feminine. XY-women have a vagina, hips and breasts. Her husband, who knew her intimately, had no idea that his wife was genetically male. It had never been told to her either, although the swimming union once knew what was going on. De Vries said, "The policy was not to inform the athlete on her condition." The union had put her on a sidetrack, avoiding confronting her with her condition. They wanted to protect her at this young age.

De Vries was one of the fastest swimmers at the breaststroke in the world. The KNZB could not really get around allowing her to compete; she was entitled to a place in the 1972 Olympic team on the basis of her performance. De Vries had been swimming at *De Watervrienden* in Amstelveen from the age of seven. She started with synchronized swimming, but at the age of fourteen she was asked to join the junior breaststroke team. When she was 21 she became a member of a professional club, *Het Y* in Amsterdam, and was selected for the national team. At the preliminaries of the Munich Games she came in third. She had already received a "beautiful Olympic swimsuit, the final phase before the Olympics." But on the evening the names of the Olympic team were announced, her name was not called. She asked the coach why but got no answer. "There I stood all alone. I have no words to describe my feelings."

The second time the KNZB passed her up was at the World Cup in Cali, Colombia, in 1973. Then again in 1974 for the World Cup in Moscow. She had dreamed of standing on the Red Square. "Later I read in a letter that I had been lucky to suffer from a knee injury." She doesn't, however, blame anyone: "I truly admire the KNZB coach and my trainer. They respected me for who I was, not disrespected me for what I am. Although it was a small world, they never told anyone what was really the matter with me."

She kept swimming and was invited to a championship in the German town of Siegen and swam, as she herself says, "out of anger a national record on the 100 meter breaststroke." Apparently she could go to championships where a gender certificate wasn't necessary. Afterwards, many years later, she discovered that the KNZB knew what was going on in 1974. Although the doctors had told her that her problems were hormonal, they apparently knew what was really at the heart of it. Her syndrome is called CAIS, which stands for Complete Androgen Insensitivity Syndrome. Women with CAIS have XY chromosomes but are immune to male hormones. Their glands make this hormone, but the cells do not respond to it. A cell has receptors that are activated by hormones, with a separate receptor for each hormone. The receptor and the hormone perfectly fit together. But when the receptor doesn't work properly, the hormone is useless, no matter how much hormones the glands produce. In CAIS the androgen receptor on the cells is defective. You could say that the key was there, but the lock was broken. Testosterone is the key that normally fits the lock, the receptor. But in CAIS, testosterone cannot open the lock. The testosterone is superfluous and is partly converted to female hormones. So the CAIS woman does get breasts, but armpit hair and pubic hair are often absent because body hair is the result of testosterone. The CAIS woman has two internal infertile testes that produce androgens, but to no effect. That is why the testes do not descend and the clitoris does not develop into a penis. The CAIS woman has no uterus or ovaries. And thus the condition often only becomes clear as the girl fails to menstruate or when a desire to have a child cannot be fulfilled.

These CAIS women are, although infertile, not ill. They are healthy women who are often good at sports, possibly because they are on the average somewhat taller and have proportionately long arms and legs. This can be a great advantage, especially in swimming and running. But it is not deemed unfair. Body length is coded by genes on the Y-chromosome. That is why men are on average taller than women.

De Vries doesn't look back in anger at the swimming union or her trainers. Although they knew what was going on, they wanted to avoid "spilling blood." She was allowed to swim at competitions that did not have compulsory sex tests. Fortunately, she did not have to go through the nightmare of being a young woman surprised and disqualified by such a radical diagnosis by an international organization that had little sympathy for the victims they made. XY-women gained access to the Olympic Games in 1992 after years of hard work by righteous people, who argued that XY-women do not have an unfair advantage provided by their high levels of male hormones. Pioneers for defending these CAIS women were Maria José Martinez Patiño and the geneticist Albert de la Chapelle.

Albert de la Chapelle, from Finland, is an expert on disorders of sexual development. One of the intersex syndromes is named after him: De la Chapelle Syndrome. Friends of mine have a son with this syndrome. When he was born his testes were not descended into the scrotum. Although in most cases there is not much to worry about, to be absolutely sure, his chromosomes were analyzed. It appeared that he had a complete set of XX-chromosomes with some DNA from the Y-chromosome; at least the SRY-gene that codes for testes. This SRY-gene was translocated from the Y- to the X-chromosome in the sperm cell of the father. Sometimes DNA travels from one chromosome to another. It's sticky material. This can cause serious trouble. In most cases this kind of pregnancy ends in a miscarriage. A de la Chapelle boy has small infertile testicles and a low testosterone level. Just like a Klinefelter, but Klinefelters have a complete Y-chromosome (47XXY). So here we have, instead of the XY-female, the XX-male. But Albert de la Chapelle can be honored for another reason. De la Chapelle was the first medical specialist who stood up against suspension of intersex athletes. He published "The Use and Misuse of Sex Chromatin Screening for 'Gender Identification' of Female Athletes."[1] In this article he states that "the present screening method is both inaccurate and discriminatory."

According to de la Chapelle a lot of harm has been done to female athletes. He wanted to put an end to this practice and offered his assistance to the CAIS athlete Maria Martinez Patiño. He had read of her case in the newspaper and came to her rescue. CAIS women, or XY-women, are the largest group of intersex athletes in athletic competition. In Atlanta 1996, eight XY-women were initially suspended. Seven of these women were completely or partially insensitive to testosterone.[2] In six of the eight women, internal testes had been removed at an earlier stage. Thanks to the protests from medical and ethical organizations, these six women got their licenses back and were allowed to participate in the Olympic Games.

The IOC initially gave the other two women a treatment plan, but they were still admitted to the Games as they were. The suspended women in 1996 all had to defend their own case before they were admitted to the Games.

For the first time in history, the IOC found it important to respect the athletes' privacy. All eight women were admitted and the sex test lost its power. In 1996, no woman was suspended. In 1999 the IOC decided to discontinue the mandatory test, though it reserved the right to use the test in so-called suspect cases.[3] In these cases the IOC would seek medical advice. That was bad news for the victims. The biggest disadvantage of this policy was that it made it harder for an athlete to fade into anonymity, especially if the test is carried out after an athlete has won a medal and is then forced to return the medal.

Just for the record: the last mandatory verification was at the Winter Games of 1998 in Nagano. Incidentally, at all Games since 2000 a fully equipped gender laboratory has been ready to investigate any suspected cases. Such a lab carries out a series of tests under the auspices of a geneticist, an endocrinologist, a psychologist and a gynecologist. In the lab itself, blood, urine and DNA from cells of the inner cheek are examined. The IAAF had discontinued sex testing in 1992. But just as the IOC did, they claimed the right to examine suspect cases. Some of the suspended women under this new regulation are discussed in the next chapter.

The IOC could have known that there was the precedent of Maria Martinez Patiño. But the Martinez Patiño case didn't lead to a new policy on CAIS. It was still "every man for himself," or better, every woman for herself. Let's take a closer look at the Martinez Patiño case.

Maria Martinez Patiño was born in July 1961. She grew up as a girl in northern Spain and she proved to excel in athletics early in her youth: running and jumping. Eventually she became a hurdler. In 1983 she received her certificate of femininity from the IAAF in Helsinki. She had passed the gender verification. In those years the femininity test was the Barr Body Test. Just to freshen your memory: in every cell with two X-chromosomes one is randomly switched off (almost completely). That X is put aside in the cell and so a woman has an active X inherited from the mother in about half of her cells and an active X chromosome inherited from the father in the other half of cells. In cases of a genetic disorder on one of the X-chromosomes, a woman can fall back on the other X (the back-up copy). In boys, genetic errors on the X always have their effect. So boys are more vulnerable to genetic disorders than girls. This explains the boy-only diseases. Boys inherited an X from their mother and don't have a back-up to rely on. The X-chromosome contains about 1,000 genes, while the Y carries instructions for male development and about 100 other genes. The Y is just a small chromosome. You're perfectly well off without it. And most certainly in the female competition. The silenced X chromosome is visible through a microscope in a dyed cell as a dark spot. The Barr Body Test, although not always reliable, can be used to get a first insight into the genetic sex of an athlete. An athlete with a Barr Body has at least two X chromosomes, one active, the other silenced, because every living human cell needs an X-chromosome. For the female competition, two X-chromosomes were necessary. The irony of the test was that men with two X's (and one Y, of course) could participate in the female competition. I already mentioned the son of my friends who has two X-chromosomes. But he would never even think about competing in the Olympics as a woman. Klinefelters XXY men would also have been able to compete as females in the second half of the last century. For they also have two X-chromosomes. They also have a deactivated X in their cells.

The IOC was enthusiastic about the Barr Body Test because in a short time you can examine many athletes cheaply and simply. You just need some cells from the inner cheek, a lab assistant with a microscope and some dye. This is where the term "chromosome" derives from—chromo means color. Chromosomes can be made visible through dyeing. The editorial staff wrote in the IOC magazine in 1968 that "a chromosome test gives a definitive answer about a person's sex." In any case, it was simple for most people to understand: under a microscope you could count sex chromosomes in a buccal smear. This meant that members of the Olympic Committee thought this test was the answer. Even medical specialists were amazed about this test, as you have read in the Schinegger biography. The miracle of modern times. So the IOC trusted the verdict of the lab. It was out of their hands. And the athletes? A major advantage of this lab test was that women no longer needed to lie spread-eagled in stirrups to be physically examined. If a woman tested negative, she left the arena under the guise of an injury. The prevailing advice was to fake an injury and take the next plane back to your hometown. And so they did. No one knew what was wrong; even the athlete didn't. But the verdict was shocking, so most left as soon as possible. Not a single athlete asked for a second opinion. But they should have, because a Barr Body Test is unreliable. The case of Maria Martinez Patiño proved this. The first Barr Body Test "proved" Martinez Patiño to be a woman, but a second test proved her to be a genetic male. Being a CAIS woman, Martinez Patiño has just one X-chromosome in her cells.

De la Chapelle's criticism of the test came at an excellent time for Maria Martinez Patiño. The Finnish geneticist offered Martinez Patiño unsolicited help to convince the IOC that their view of sex was fundamentally incorrect, that their test was not reliable. In 1983 Martinez Patiño got her gender certificate. The result was: woman. She ran at the World Championships in Helsinki in 1983 on the 100-meter hurdles. Her time was 13.78. Two years later, in 1985, she participated as a student in the World University Games in Kobe, Japan. Something dramatic happened there. She forgot to bring her gender certificate with her to Japan so the test had to be repeated. In the laboratory there the experts could not see a Barr Body in her cells. Martinez Patiño told her own story in *The Lancet*:

> Later that day, our team doctor told me—in front of the teammates I sat with on the night before my race—that there was a problem with my result. At the hospital the next day, I learned that a sophisticated karyotype analysis would be undertaken, and that the results would take months to reach my sports federation in Spain. I would be unable to compete in that day's race. Our team doctor advised me to consult with a specialist when I got home, and urged me in the meantime to fake an injury, so that no one would suspect anything untoward. I was shocked, but did as I was told. I sat in the stands that day watching my teammates, wondering how my body differed from theirs. I spent the rest of that week in my room, feeling a sadness that I could not share. My mind spun: did I have AIDS? Or leukemia, the disease that had killed my brother?[4]

Maria José Martinez Patiño

This goes to show how a little bit of bad luck has the potential to ruin your career. Had she taken her certificate to Japan, she would have been able to go to the 1988 Games in Seoul, South Korea, and perhaps to take an Olympic medal back to Spain. In the end, further testing showed that she should have been entitled to go to Seoul to compete. Two months later, after visiting several doctors all alone—because her parents were still grieving for her brother—she received the verdict: All of the 50 counted cells by Giemsa Staining had 46 chromosomes. Karyotype analysis by Q-banding method revealed her sex chromosome constitution is XY. Karyotype is decided 46, XY. Martinez Patiño said, "I have androgen insensitivity, and don't respond to testosterone. When I was conceived, my tissues never heard the hormonal messages to become male."

Although she must have suspected that there was something medically wrong with her, she never saw herself as a man, and she never intended to. She was not even planning to accept her suspension. In spite of the test she still wanted to qualify for the Olympic Games, and would try to do so through the 1986 national championship in Spain. At the start, the referee asked her to leave on penalty of public disqualification. Martinez Patiño however did not intend to back off, so she ran her match and was then disqualified. The athletics association in Spain leaked her condition to the press. She was no longer allowed to enter the athletics track and field, and lost her scholarship and the man she would marry. "I lost my hope and my energy. But I knew that I was a woman and that my genotype did not offer me an unfair advantage. I can hardly pretend to be a man. I have breasts and a vagina." Maria Martinez Patiño could indeed not benefit from her syndrome. She is completely insensitive to testosterone. But she lost everything nevertheless—"as if I had never existed."

But in the end she took the right steps. Speculations about her gender stopped. And she cleared the way for other CAIS women to participate in the Olympics. As of 1992 no CAIS woman was stopped by the IOC. Just as Carla de Vries is, Maria Martinez Patiño is a CAIS woman. A woman with a male Y-chromosome. Due to the Y the indifferent gonads of the embryo become testes. The testosterone the testes release has no effect on further masculinization. So the testes do not descend, and no penis is formed. The embryo remains as it is predisposed: appearance girl (but with the potential to become a girl or a boy). A girl with a vagina and a clitoris. The vagina is usually shallow. Obviously, there are no ovaries. When a CAIS girl is born, she looks completely feminine.

This syndrome disrupted the gender verification policy of the IOC at the end of the 1980s. Until then, it was assumed that women with a Y-chromosome had an unfair advantage over other women because of high testosterone levels in the blood. They were stronger, more muscular. But the vast majority of intersex athletes were CAIS and thus could not benefit from one of the several functions of testosterone: muscle building. The hormone is superfluous for these women and so there is no unfair advantage. It took more than two decades before the IOC realized this fact, but the indications were there.

Martinez Patiño was the first athlete who formally protested against her suspension, with the support of Albert de la Chapelle. He had been very negative in publications about gender verification in sports. Tests were unethical, discriminating and unreliable, he said. With his expertise, Martinez Patiño managed to get her license again. The decision took three years, however; a long time to wait. The medical committee of the IOC discussed the Martinez Patiño case in Seoul 1988. The IAAF director, Arne Ljungqvist, personally sent her the license. "I had paid a high price for it," Martinez Patiño wrote in *The Lancet*. However, in the preliminaries of the 1992 Olympics, she was one tenth of a second short. Her license came too late; a lot of valuable time had been wasted. But she had won another important battle for many other sportswomen, even though it took until 2012 before the IOC formally adjusted the regulations for CAIS women. In the meantime, every CAIS sportswoman still had to fight personally to get her license back.

It was remarkable that when the Indian athlete Dutee Chand objected at the Court of Arbitrage for Sports (CAS) against the testosterone limit, Martinez Patiño was an advocate for the IAAF. According to her, there is always someone who has an advantage in sport so there must be clear rules for all athletes. I found it very disappointing to read in the interim report of the Chand case that Martinez Patiño supported the IAAF in their claim that a high T gave hyperandrogenic women an unfair benefit (when they are sensitive to testosterone). Martinez Patiño is a scientist at the University of Vigo in Spain so she should have known that you need scientific evidence before you take far-reaching decisions on women. There was no scientific research done on the benefits of endogenous—natural—testosterone in women athletes. Therefore the CAS decided justly to postpone the rules for two years.[5]

Martinez Patiño said, "We did not expect this statement." Still, Martinez Patiño does feel a bond with hyperandrogenic athletes like Caster Semenya and Dutee Chand: "We are being stigmatized. We are also different sportswomen and live in a different time."

For the future of gender verification, one question is actually more relevant than T-levels: how can it be that a relatively large number of CAIS women are so good at sports like running and swimming? It is possible that these athletes have a biological advantage other than testosterone? Worldwide 1 in 40,000 births is an XY woman with CAIS. In sport, 1 in 400 to 450 athletes is androgen insensitive. So there are relatively many CAIS women active in elite sports. We know this from the number of suspensions from 1972 Munich to 1996 Atlanta.[6] The number is pretty constant. It follows that far more CAIS women are active in elite sports than you can expect based on the number of births. There is a factor of 140. What makes these women so fast? It is not their strength, we know that. The muscle strength is not enhanced by testosterone. Is it the physique? It is high time to no longer wonder whether testosterone significantly improves performance. It is time to investigate why CAIS women perform so well, especially in athletics. In any case, Atlanta statistics show that they are taller on average. XY women also have a favorable lean body mass, which is the body weight minus the fat. IOC does not consider such factors unfair. But height and fat percentage do matter in many sports.[7]

Blackmail and Suicide

On October 9, 2001, a distraught young woman tied bags filled with stones to her ankles and jumped into the village well. She had just received a disturbing phone call and left her home in tears. The next morning the villagers fished her dead body out of the deep well. This was the all-time low of sex testing.

Her name was Pratima Gaonkar and she would have been forgotten completely had her brother not decided to tell her story ten years after her tragic death. This was in the weeks that another Indian intersex athlete was being blackmailed. Gaonkar's family normally avoided the media. They didn't like to speak about her tragic death. It was too difficult, even after ten years.

Gaonkar has just a handful of Google hits and no Wikipedia page. She should be remembered. Her story remains important in the history of gender testing. There are lessons to be learned from her death.

Pratima Gaonkar held great athletic promise for India in the 400 meters. The people of the Indian state of Goan called her the "new PT Usha," who was a beloved Indian track and field athlete who won many gold and silver medals at the Asian Games.[1] Her most famous quote is: "I never wanted to be an Olympian. All I wanted was to keep breaking my own record. I never competed to defeat anybody."[2]

Pratima was to follow in PT Usha's footsteps. Usha had already accepted that Pratima, a year after Usha's retreat from track and field, was faster. Usha had finished her astonishing and long career (1980–2000) and found a formidable successor in Pratima Gaonkar. Her legacy seemed secure.

Pratima was 17 years old when she bagged five gold medals at the West Zone Meet (Indian junior matches). At the age of 19 she won a silver medal at the Asian Junior Games on the 4 × 400 relay. She was the first athlete from the Indian State of Goan to participate in one of the biggest athletic

events in the world: the Asian Junior Athletic Games in July 2001 in Brunei. These games for athletes under 20 are held every two years. The name
Pratima Gaonkar still stands in the medal book. And on some yellowed
newspaper clippings in the family album. But as you might guess by now,
Pratima was tested for those games. It was later learned she had a gender
"problem."

We are led to believe that intersex people in India are called "the third
sex" and are accepted in the community. If you know how hard it is for a
woman to survive in India, you would realize that intersex people are just
as neglected in India as everywhere else in the world. I don't think there's
any region in the world were intersex women are accepted. It's just wishful
thinking. There's no intersex paradise.

As a successful athlete Pratima was the hope of the family, which had
been surviving on her mother's income of 15 rupees a day as a farm hand.
Her father, a miner, had died six years earlier. During the week Pratima
was at her training facility, but upon returning home on the weekends she
first visited the food market to buy enough food for the coming week for
her mother and siblings. The family finally now had enough to eat, and a
balanced diet at that, thanks to Pratima's talent.

Her mother had noticed the physical changes that took place when
her daughter reached the age of 13 or 14. But she never spoke with Pratima
on what she later called "hormone changes."[3] Like almost all other intersex
girls of that time, Pratima was left to her fate. They were on their own to
sort out their gender problems, all the while nearly always thinking that
they were the only girl in the world with this puzzling condition. Pratima
had to cope all alone with her deep, dark secret. And maybe the shame was
so overwhelming that it was impossible for her to speak about her condition with anybody. But she had the moral right of being counseled by the
athletic union after the sex test. She needed help. But they abandoned her.
I don't think there ever was a road map for the aftercare of suspended athletes. In earlier days the federations were glad to get rid of them. And even
as the sports federations started to realize that the athletes did not distort
the competition on purpose, they got the opportunity to leave the competition through the back door, and the door was closed after they left. They
were left to themselves. They even lost their friends from the sports teams.

I know from the case of the Dutchwoman Foekje Dillema that the
Dutch Union tried to contact her 45 years after her suspension. They sent
her a letter and a bunch of flowers. In the letter she was invited to talk about

the day she was barred. The intentions were good, but much too late. Foekje did not react to the invitation. Too little, too late.

After the sex test results, Pratima decided to resolve her intersex condition through surgery. She had saved the money for the operation. But during this period she began receiving disturbing phone calls. According to Pratima's mother, someone wanted to blackmail her and demanded Rs 50,000.[4] The theory is that the man who started blackmailing her knew the outcome of the gender verification. Perhaps someone inside the Indian Athletic Union had read the report on the results of the sex test. The main suspect is her coach. He was transferred to the regional office of the Sports Authority of India at Gandhinagar for further inquiry. It was learned that on October 8, the day before her death, Pratima went to the bank in Mapusa, accompanied by a village friend and her coach, and withdrew Rs 5,000. This day was a national holiday in India.

According to Pratima's mother it was her coach who made the phone call the next day asking for more money. Her coach vehemently denied the allegation of blackmailing Pratima, claiming that he had helped Pratima financially from time to time.[5]

In the end nobody was convicted for blackmailing Gaonkar. To this day nobody knows for sure who made the phone call. But there can be no doubt that the call came from inside the Indian Athletic Union. If the union was careless with the report on Pratima's sex development, they are responsible.

After the phone call Pratima "lost her religion." According to her mother she was crying as she ended the call with the pleading words: "Sir, you can't do this." This was what her mother told the police in her statement: "she was wracked with worry the days before her suicide." The phone call will probably swirl round in the heads of her mother and brother for the rest of their lives.

Newslaundry reported: "At the time of her suicide, Pratima was on her way to the peak of her power. She had broken all state track and field records, knocked down some records at the zonal and national athletics meets, and had even helped India win a silver medal on 4x400 meter relay in the Sultanate of Brunei. An Olympic medal was next on her menu."

But Pratima's life ended in the village well. Just 19 years old. End of story? No. At a press conference a senior superintendent of police revealed the contents of the dead athlete's postmortem. The postmortem, conducted by Dr. Avinash Pujari, had revealed that Pratima had a male organ measuring half an inch, while female organs like ovaries, uterus and vagina were missing. The report also said that her breasts were not fully developed. Even after her death Pratima Gaonkar was dishonored. The press conference went into history as "the two-inch penis theory." This conference was of course superfluous. There was no need to share this private information with the general public. The humiliating news was on the front pages of the newspapers. The sports authorities of Goan promised—to ease their conscience—Pratima's brother Shivanand a job as soon as he finished his studies. He did, but the sports authorities never kept their promise. News on Pratima slowly slipped out of the newspapers. Everyone forgot about the athlete and her tragic death. Did the national and international athletic union learn from this heartbreaking incident? No! They just don't seem to know what is happening at ground level. They don't seem to realize what impact a negative sex test has on a young girl. There almost never was any aftercare. And suspension of intersex athletes continued. But it's contrary to the values we like to uphold in sports like uniting the people, like participating being more important than winning, like sports being a basic human right. For Pratima Gaonkar, participating again was worse than winning.

Three years later, in the final days of 2004 there was a scuffle at the Habibpur station in Ranaghat, India. The 18-year-old runner Pinki Pramanik hit one of the five boys who were bothering her. The boys grabbed Pinki at her wrists and dragged her to the police station. Pramanik declared that the boys were harassing her and that she had beaten one. The boys were told to wait outside the office, but they ran off and were never heard of again. The police investigated Pinki's luggage and found in her travel bag a homemade weapon, with which you can fire one bullet. Pramanik said she found the weapon in the bathroom at the station. The police did not trust her.

Pinki had disappeared without a trace a month before. She left her training camp and apparently stayed with friends in Habibpur. The police wanted to know why she didn't hand over the weapon to the railway management. Pinki gave a confusing statement and was only released after two days. Unfortunately, it was not the last time that Pramanik came into contact with the police. She was a sportswoman who had been treated harshly and was humiliated by the government, the IAAF and physicians.

We've arrived in the 21st century. After the IOC and the IAAF abolished the mandatory gender verification, there were still the suspicious cases. In India alone this included at least three athletes. India is poor in lots of regions. People live far away from hospitals. And nobody talks about gender problems. We know of the Indian cases because the right to privacy there is systematically violated.

There seems to be no rule of confidentiality by doctors. And maybe because Pinki Pramanik got herself in all sorts of trouble there was never a dull moment with her. She was never mellow and laid back, and was assertive, to say the least. But her right to physical integrity was severely violated.

The runner Pramanik comes, like so many other intersex athletes, from the countryside. Her father was a poor farmer. She was born on April 10, 1986, in Purulia, a district in West Bengal in northeastern India. Her real name is Jyotsna, which means "moonlight," but because she was pink as a baby, they called her "Pinki." And that would always be her nickname. Pinki is one of five daughters in the Pramanik family and grew up, just like her sisters, as a girl. Her mother later rejected all speculation about Pinki's gender: "She is exactly the same as my other four daughters."[6] Pinki was considered a girl at the time of her birth. A midwife delivered her but there's no birth certificate. We do not know whether physical changes occurred during puberty and of which the mother would know nothing. It's certainly possible. A late onset of male characteristics is possible in several syndromes. One these syndromes is IAIS,[7] Incomplete Androgen Insensitivity Syndrome. Four Olympic female athletes were diagnosed IAIS in 1996.[8] It is possible that Pinki Pramanik has IAIS. And perhaps Pratima Gaonkar as well?

What is IAIS? Remember Martinez Patiño was CAIS, with the C standing for "complete." There is however a group of XY-women who are not completely insensitive to androgens. Male hormones have a mild effect on their cells. They are partially sensitive to androgen. IAIS can lead to several gender conditions, but we can rest assured that female athletes with this condition were born and raised as girls and therefore can join the female competition. But at puberty they virilized to a certain degree due to a new cascade of male hormones.

They were born female because the reaction to androgens was too weak for them to develop into boys before birth. Their external genitals appeared to be female. The testes that were formed in the seventh week of pregnancy produced testosterone and stronger androgens, but insensitivity to this hormone disrupts the formation of the external sex organs before birth. During puberty, the second cascade of hormones leads to the development of secondary sex characteristics but only to a certain degree. These characteristics include an increased muscle mass, pubic hair, deepening of the voice, and possibly an enlarged clitoris. Incomplete Androgen Insensitivity Syndrome results in the partial inability of the cell to respond to androgens. In IAIS the sex chromosomes are XY. The T-level is high but has a limited effect. My assumption is that Pinki Pramanik is an IAIS-woman. Why? Because of her life story.

Born a girl—that is where Pinki's life story starts. She was raised a girl and had a talent for running. She was always running. As an adolescent Pinki worked with the Eastern Railways. The long-distance train is the main means of transportation in West Bengal. She was a ticket collector, someone who cuts the tickets, but was not responsible for boarding and disembarking. The Eastern Railways supported her in her sports. The railway company gave her regular paid leave to train for or run in competitions.

The first time Pinki competed formally was in Jharkhand in 2000. She won medals and received a cow and a goat as gifts from the organizers.[9] The story doesn't say what she did with the livestock.

Pinki specialized in middle-distances: the 400 and the 800 meters. She won a silver medal at the relay at the Commonwealth Games in Melbourne and in the same year, 2006, three gold medals at the Asian Games. She was selected to represent India at the IAAF World Games. She came in seventh, at only 17 years old. She then held the Asian youth records at the four distances: 100, 200, 400 and 800 meters. There is much more on her honor roll, but these are the most important achievements. At 17 she was India's most promising young athlete. But she was not always a nice competitor. Her fellow athletes report a history of "rough behavior" and how she "lived on the edge," though there was little elaborating. She was called a "late-nighter who enjoyed the good things in life."[10] But she could also be aggressive and even her teammates seemed to be afraid of her. They only wanted to talk in anonymity about Pramanik. The *Times of India* quoted a female competitor: "'We all felt there was something wrong with her,' but no one ever complained or openly questioned Pinki's gender, ostensibly because she was very aggressive. Only once, it is learnt, a complaint was lodged against Pinki when she 'over-performed' during the heats of a tournament."

"A sex determination test was scheduled but Pinki ducked it by pulling out of the competition," said a coach, who also didn't want his name in the newspaper.

Still, it remains unclear whether she was tested by the national union or the IAAF at that time. Her detractors are convinced that her sudden disappearance in 2007 is evidence that she was quietly pulled out of the competition by the Athletic Federation of India.

The secretary of the West Bengal Federation told the press that "Pinki retired from competitive events after an ankle injury in Doha." But we know announcing an injury was the standard procedure in gender suspensions. So I wouldn't be surprised if she had been tested.

We would never have known the truth about her disputed gender, if she wasn't such a controversial person. She just couldn't stay out of the newspapers. Her face was constantly on the front pages of the popular press. She was tested—not by the IAAF because of possible gender fraud—but by the public prosecutors after an accusation of rape. This is the upsetting story that hit all the headlines in India.

Pinki shared her apartment with a girlfriend, although she herself claimed that it was her former neighbor whom she took into her home out of compassion. This former neighbor—who remained anonymous in the press—had been abandoned by her husband. Pinki claimed that her live-in partner paid rent. It is, however, much more likely that she and Pinki had an affair. In June 2012, the friendship derailed. Her estranged partner/roommate talked about how Pramanik "cheated the whole world" by posing as a female athlete.[11] On top of it she accused Pramanik of raping her. Pinki's side of the story was that her roommate had taken nude photos of her in order to blackmail her. They were not the perfect couple. The roommate also accused Pinki of being the man who promised to marry her. A complex relationship, to say the least. Pinki denied all charges, saying, "I am not a man. I look more masculine because I train to participate in elite international athletics competitions. In addition, like all ladies, I regularly received 'Russian medication.' They said I needed it and I never wondered if it was legal. I did what was necessary to win. But because of those injections, my voice has dropped and I got more body hair."[12] "Russian medication" is a euphemism for synthetic testosterone. That Pinki became more masculine through this "medication" seems obvious. But keep in mind that synthetic testosterone has different qualities and effects than natural testosterone.[13]

Women usually only make small amounts of testosterone in the ovaries and the adrenal glands. Testosterone improves the libido in men and women. That's one of the reasons women have a low testosterone level. Too much testosterone, however, makes women hyperandrogenic, which leads to masculinity. Russian medicine deepens the voice, increases body hair, strengthens muscles and can result in enlarging the clitoris. There seem to be no effects on social behaviors. Aggression is not a result of a high testosterone level. Women should be careful in using synthetic testosterone.

On June 24, 2012, Pinki was arrested on the accusation of rape and was held in the male ward of the Dum Dum Correctional Home. The public prosecutor had decided that she was male, because in those days, rape was only punishable if a penis was inserted into a vagina by force and against the will of the female person. Indian law was very specifically formulated. Rape is only punishable when a man rapes a woman. The authorities did not give her the benefit of the doubt. So now Pinki had two related problems on her hands: an accusation of rape and the accusation that she is a man. The first, under Indian law, one cannot do without the second. It is quite complicated. Pinki had to be examined physically, and the question had to be answered about whether she was able to penetrate a woman with a penis. This investigation took place in no fewer than three hospitals, because there was no one sufficient facility in the state of West Bengal to answer the complex question adequately. In one of the hospitals, an employee used his mobile phone to film the moment that Pinki was naked and being tested by the doctors. This 29-second video went online. Pinki went viral.[14] It was unheard of. On top of it she lost her job with Eastern Railways.

The first two hospitals were unable to provide a satisfactory answer to the question about the sex of Pinki on the basis of a physical examination. So a chromosome analysis had to be performed. Pinki said about these tests that she had never given her permission and that she had been put to sleep with medication in the clinics. "When I woke up, I was naked and tied hands and feet to the bed."[15] Her physical integrity was brutally violated. But her privacy too: "We have conducted all kinds of necessary medical tests on her, whatever is possible considering the highest medical infrastructure as per the Indian standards. This much I can tell you that Pinki is not 'she'— neither genetically nor anatomically," a senior member of the SSKM medical board told *Mail Today* (SSKM is a state hospital).[16]

The medical panel had conducted various tests, such as on blood samples and other clinical tests, like MRI, ultrasonography, hormonal study, and chromosomal test or karyotyping. "The athlete has many predominant male features from both the chromosomal and anatomical aspects," a forensic expert, who was a member of the medical board, said. "Pinki has 46 XY karyotype which is normally common in a male body." And: "Pinki is a 'male pseudo-hermaphrodite.'" Yes, this is in 2012. This is medicine in India. The persistent breach of professional secrecy would be unacceptable in the West.

What is a male pseudo-hermaphrodite? Geneticists in particular distinguish between a "true hermaphrodite" and a "pseudo-hermaphrodite." That is all dated diagnostic terminology, but on the internet these terms are still used as well as in some medical circuits. And in the Pinki case you always come across this diagnosis. A true hermaphrodite has both testicular and ovarian tissue. This can be a testicle in combination with an ovary. It can also include gonads that contain both ovarian and testicular tissue (ovotestes). This does not mean that a true hermaphrodite is also capable of reproducing along both the female and male line. A pseudo-hermaphrodite is a person that is born with primary sex characteristics of one sex but develops the secondary sex characteristics of the other sex. A male pseudo-hermaphrodite has testes and female secondary sex characteristics. So Pinki has testes and female secondary sex characteristics. There are a lot of misconceptions associated with these terms. That is why I prefer the term intersex. A person in between sexes. According to the gynecologist Gautam Khastagir, Pinki has "an undeveloped phallus, internal testicles and no vagina or uterus. Her sexual identity is ambiguous."[17] This is the reason why the Calcutta High Court acquitted her of rape. The karyotyping was done unnecessarily. The diagnosis of the gynecologist was sufficient to answer the legal question. But they went all the way with Pramanik. She was released after 26 days. It has never been clear what exactly happened between the two "friends." Of course there are conspiracy theories about this. I'd rather let that pass.

She reluctantly told the inquisitive press: "I am not a man, I am a woman, always been, I looked cute as a child, I wore girl's clothes, I have been in love with a man, a fellow athlete. I have however decided not to marry." When the journalist asked her how she was feeling, she replied: "I have given myself house arrest, I do not want to go outside and show my face. I feel naked."[18] Meanwhile, many people protested, especially the women's movements. Why was Pinki locked up in a men's prison? How could there have been private camera recordings in a hospital? Why did the police—you can see it on the internet—go for her breasts? Why were no female agents deployed in her arrest? Why was Pinki—who officially lived as a woman—not considered a woman? Pinki was humiliated in every way possible. Her private life was out on the street. In India, however, no one ever officially protested.

So Pinki was 46XY. Having internal testes, she was hyperandrogenic, but only mildly reacted to androgens like testosterone. And being born a girl, her "undeveloped phallus" must have been the result of the surge of male hormones during puberty. Maybe the Russian medicine also contributed to the virilization. In 2007 the Y-chromosome was the key factor for suspension for life. If Pramanik was suspended that year it must have been a result of having a Y-chromosome.

Nine months after the acquittal, Pinki bought new running shoes. She tried to come back to the track, applying for a license at the athletics federation. But she didn't get one. She didn't even receive an answer. It undoubtedly had to do with the results of the femininity tests. The Indian Athletic Union probably did not intend to let her run. But Pinki was not the person to back down so easily. She asked her employer and sponsor, Eastern Railways, to let her train. Her sponsor had always been kind to her. But she did not receive an answer here either. Pinki said, "Although I have always been treated with respect by Eastern Railways, even during my arrest, I am now hindered to return to the competition circuit." She called it discrimination. Jyotsna Mukherjee, Eastern Railways' sports official, denied that they discriminated against Pinki: "She has passed her height. We now have three or four girls who are in a much better form. Pinki Pramanik will first have to prove at local level before returning to the national level. If she improves, we will give her training opportunities."[19]

But even at the local level, she needed permission from her sponsor. Pinki claimed that she should be entitled to more respect, because "she was sportswoman of the year in 2006 and 2007." But for a sportswoman in 2012, that was a long time ago. I think we can also reasonably assume that her genetic makeup played a major role in this issue. She would not get a start license. She would be obliged to take testosterone inhibitors before she could get a license. From 2012 on, such a cure was mandatory for hyperandrogenic women.

Pinki Pramanik tried to reach for Rio in 2016, the Olympic year when she was allowed to start without hormone therapy. Pinki decided to fight back: "Nobody supported me when I went through a crisis. I was left to my fate, but I am determined to come back." She was now thirty years old. She took three months of unpaid leave and paid all expenses herself. Her ambition was a place on the 4 × 400 relay team. But she didn't get her chance; her athletic performance was just not good enough.

Pinki Pramanik was not the only intersex runner who excelled at the

"They say I'm not a girl"

Asian Games in Qatar in 2006. Her compatriot Santhi Soundarajan won a silver medal in the 800 meters. Soundarajan is Tamil, a population with its own language and culture. Tamils live in various countries, including India and Sri Lanka. Santhi also belongs to the caste of the Dalits, the untouchables, or, rather, the group that is excluded from the caste system. Dalits are at the very bottom of the social system. Every physical contact with the Dalits is abhorred. This has nothing to do with hygiene; they are unclean in a religious sense. It is a degrading system.

Santhi Soundarajan was born in April 1981 in a 20- by 5-meter hut, without gas, electricity and running water, in a village called Aalangaadu. As the eldest daughter she took care of her siblings. Her parents were brick-kiln laborers in a rural village in southern Tamil Nadu. They earned the equivalent of four American dollars a week. It comes as no surprise that Santhi had to overcome malnutrition she suffered as a child.

Soundarajan was trained by her athletic grandfather. He taught her to run on an open stretch of dirt outside the hut and bought her a pair of running shoes. At her first competition, in eighth grade, Soundarajan won a tin cup trophy. It would be one of many trophies. The sports coach at a nearby high school took note of her performance and recruited her. The school paid her tuition and provided her with a uniform and hot lunches. It was the first time Soundarajan had ever eaten three meals a day.[20] Through running she could escape from poverty.

The Asian Games are a big event because many large countries—India, China, Indonesia, Japan and Korea—participate. These games are organized every four years, just like the Olympic Games. Her parents couldn't afford a television so they watched their daughter running in the Games at a neighbor's house.

The regional government of Sri Lanka and the Tamils themselves are proud of their "daughter"; for the first time a Tamil won a silver medal at the Asian Games, where she clocked 2 minutes 3.16 seconds. Although the admiration of the Tamils is permanent, Santhi lost her medals after the Games in Qatar. "I'm left with nothing but broken dreams," Santhi said in 2016. The Olympic Council of Asia stripped Santhi of the silver medal; she was "disqualified as per the recommendations of the medical committee on a Games rule violation." The Indian Olympic Association (IOA) said the 25-year-old had failed a sex test.[21] The test disputed her eligibility. According to the test "she does not possess the sexual characteristics of a woman."[22] The instigation of the sex test seems to have come from a doping control official. In doubtful cases the IAAF can request an athlete to take a gender test. They did.

The Indian Athletic Federation drew her blood and examined her body. Soundarajan was examined by a team of doctors including a gynecologist, a geneticist and a psychologist. They did not speak Tamil, her native language. She was examined for 30 minutes and then the doctors left the room. The next day she was told to leave the Games, without explanation. Santhi was suspended from the female division.[23] The disqualification was, according to the *New York Times Magazine*, leaked to the press at large. Soundarajan was watching a sports match on television when she heard that she had "failed a sex test."[24] The news was beamed on all channels: "She is not a woman and stripped of her medals." Santhi stared at the screen in shock. It was there for the whole world to see: she failed a gender verification. She lost everything—the support of the sports federations, her medals, her records, her dignity.

Santhi said, "I was completely defeated by this news, the Indian League did not support me. I had the hope that they would support me. I feel like I have lost everything. I am very depressed."[25] The Indian Athletics Federation even felt that Santhi had inflicted shame on her country.

Ten years later she said in a video that she couldn't live a normal life after the test results were broadcast. "They always look at me differently." Before the disqualification she dressed as a woman, but people talked behind her back in a way that hurt her. She cut her hair and changed her dressing style, so people wouldn't know who she was.[26]

The secretary of the Indian Olympic Committee did not want to tell her more than she could never run again. When asked why, the secretary only said on the mobile phone, "it was confirmed, she was not allowed to complete anymore."[27] Her coach told her that "her condition had arisen because she had been undernourished as a child." This is nonsense, of course.

The *New York Times Magazine*, a well-informed journal, wrote that Santhi is CAIS, completely insensitive to male hormones.[28] But is she? I'm not sure, because her condition was reported by a doping official. These officials observe the athlete while they provide their urine sample. The doping official may have noticed something that made her doubt the gender of Soundarajan. In CAIS the external genitals would be completely female. There would be no reason to doubt her gender. IAIS is therefore more likely than CAIS. Does it matter? Yes, because with CAIS she could have been cleared the same day and returned to the competition, without treatment. Just like Maria Martinez Patiño.

The Indian Federation does not intend to help her in any way. It doesn't help that Shanti belongs to the Dalits. It is fixed at your birth to which caste you belong. Dalits do the dirtiest and heaviest work in India. Indians of other castes do not want to touch anything touched by a Dalit. Even a thoroughly washed cup is unclean. The government is trying—so far, in vain—to change this system. But the difficulty is that it is a religious system that comes from the sacred books, the Vedas. The Dalits also accept their fate for religious reasons. Even more problematic than the system at large is how it doesn't work at all for Dalit women. They have no control over life and body. Within such a degrading system it is inconceivable that anyone would stand by a woman like Santhi. She was completely alone. After her suspension, she had no other choice than to work with her parents in the brickworks.

Santhi tried to find work at her level, but all attempts failed. She had been extensively in the press and was portrayed as a disgrace to the country. In the end, Santhi, like her parents, started working as a day laborer in a brick factory for 200 rupees a day. This is the wage for women and is lower than for men. So when it comes to money she suddenly was a woman after all! This work consists of mixing stone powder with clay and water, damaging her hands. "In the beginning I could not do anything with my hands after work. I could not even eat. Sometimes I think about committing suicide, or moving to a place where nobody knows me. What did I do wrong? Why am I being punished for something that I have no control over?" The tone of this conversation was disturbing. This was also the period in which she tried to end her life. She was so depressed that she had not succeeded in finding a way back to athletics or even into society. She was "physically and mentally completely broken." She did not want to talk about it anymore. On September 5, 2007, she attempted suicide, probably with a veterinary pesticide. A friend found her vomiting uncontrollably and brought her to a hospital.

Hindustan Times reported:

Athlete Santhi Soundarajan, who failed a gender test after winning a silver medal in the Doha Asian Games last year, on Wednesday allegedly attempted suicide by consuming some veterinary medicines. Santhi was admitted to a hospital in Pudukottai and was now out of danger, police said.

Shanthi is able to speak and she has denied that she attempted suicide. She maintains that she took some medicines for stomach pain. The doctors, who attended on her, however said she had consumed veterinary medicines.

It's said that it is always darkest before the dawn. Ultimately, there was someone who stood up for her: the popular politician Jayaraman Jayalithaa, known among the Tamils as Amma, a former actress who went into politics after her film career ended. She acted in 140 Indian films and is therefore famous and very popular in India. Amma was then the chief minister of Tamil Nadu when she awarded Santhi a scholarship and money to use to start her own training center. It was the not inconsiderable amount of $30,000. It must have given her enormous satisfaction. Now Santhi was running her own sports academy with around 70 students. She rented a house where ten top talents from the poorest families could stay and she lives there herself. She runs that hostel with her own income from the training facility. "I know what it's like to be poor. I even begged for food as a child. When I started training I got food from my coach. I'm doing the same for my students now."

Santhi hoped to be able to go to Rio in 2016, but was already 35 years old and long past her best times. She added: "My legacy will not stay with my medals, but I will have to overcome my past struggles. I want to live my dream through my students."[29] She wants to be remembered as an athlete who was determined to win her battle.

Santhi is still fighting to get her medals back, with support from the Tamil government. I'm afraid she's going to lose that fight. If the IOC and IAAF were to finally change the rules for intersex athletes, many, many athletes could claim the return of their records and medals, from Foekje Dillema (posthumously, of course) to Santhi Soundarajan. Others would have to hand in their medals again. The organizations will never agree to that, I fear. A new regulation will only apply to future athletes. The rest are, unfortunately, covered by the old regulations.

Sarah Gronert

Tennis Anyone?

The first thing that comes to mind, looking at tennis player Sarah Gronert, is: "What a beautiful woman!" And that is probably the key to her story. Why? Because her gender story was just a marginal issue in the news compared to the allegations made against her contemporary Caster Semenya.

It's sometimes hard to imagine that CAIS women like Gronert are intersex. Compared with her, androgen sensitive athletes provoke more doubt and more hostility. People tend to regard these athletes as male frauds. At 19 Sarah Gronert underwent surgery that made her eligible for the female tennis tour. She was born intersex with male and female sexual characteristics. The surgery was only mentioned in the margins of the newspapers. This was striking because gender operations in sports nearly always get a lot of attention in the serious and in the popular press. Was this because seeing her you just can't imagine that she's a genetic male?

Someone—and I forgot who—once said that CAIS women are the most beautiful women in the world. That's an exaggeration of course, but if they are good looking, they have this little extra perk: perfect skin. "And it covers my whole body," Annie Hall would add. They are good at sports, and sometimes make perfect models for ads and fashion magazines. It's because they have long legs, thick hair, perfect skin and ample breasts. One of these intersex models is the Belgian Hanne Gaby Odiele who came out publicly in *Vogue*. Odiele said, "For a lot of people the first time they hear about it, is when they talk to me. They have no idea. There's a kind of shame placed on our bodies, like we are not supposed to talk about it." She went on: "I will never know what it is to be a cisgender woman, I will never be able to talk about a period or having a child, but I'm not a man either—I'm proud intersex. I was born with internal testes that produce testosterone, but which my body converts to estrogen. It's crazy, right!"

Odiele spent a period of her youth in and out of hospitals. Her parents followed the advice of doctors and made a gender choice for her. She knew, as she says now, that "the body she was born with is gone." Surgery is irreversible. The current Western opinion is that surgery to make the genitals look "more normal" shouldn't be performed until the child is mature enough to decide for him or herself. "There is no evidence that children who grow up with intersex genitals are worse off psychologically than those who are altered."[1]

Finding out at a later stage in her life that she was intersex came both as a shock and as a relief: "I always felt I was the only one like me, that I had this weird thing going on. I just don't understand why we need to fix something that is not broken. There nothing wrong with being a bit different."

Shortly after Odiele found out about herself she began pursuing a career as model, which is possibly the most female-centric job in the world. "I felt I was playing the system a little bit," she said. Odiele married John Swiatek, a DJ and model and the pair adopted a son. Familiar with the question regarding gender-neutral pronouns, Odiele said: "I don't feel female and don't feel male, but I like 'she.'"[2]

According to endocrinologist Norman Spack, "There are several prominent actresses today in America—I can't reveal their names—who have CAIS."[3] It's always the same names of sexy actresses that pop up. It's because they have this androgynous appeal (per film critic Bill Cosford). The actresses themselves never comment on gender questions. But I'm sure that in the film and music industry there are and have been famous CAIS women. Coming out is still difficult. It's such private information, for themselves and their spouses.

No, it's not my place to judge the beauty of sportswomen. I'm just including this because the beauties get away with it more easily than masculine intersex women like Semenya. Sarah Gronert is not world famous because of her intersex condition, like Caster Semenya is. Compared to the storm Semenya unwillingly provoked, there was just a gentle breeze in the Gronert case.

Gronert was born July 6, 1986, in Germany, in a small town called Linnich. She grew into a tall, blonde girl of 1.83 meters (about 6 feet) with a ferocious tennis serve. She underwent surgery at the age of 19. *The Telegraph* reported in March 2009:

"They say I'm not a girl"

A female professional player who was born with both male and female genitalia has had her case reviewed by a Women's Tennis Association Tour "medical delegate" to make sure that she satisfied all the requirements to compete in the women's game. The delegate concluded that there was "sufficient independent and verifiable evidence" to show that Sarah Gronert, a 22-year-old German, was eligible to play women's tennis. Under the WTA Tour's rules, if there is "any question as to the eligibility" of a player, the WTA has the right to "require a player to submit to gender verification to determine sexual status."

Gronert should be applauded for having had the courage to carry on playing, having rightly decided that she was going to make the most of her talent, and this season she has made good progress with her career, winning two titles on the International Tennis Federation's (ITF) women's circuit, which is just below the main WTA Tour.

The local and national South African athletic unions betrayed Semenya (as will be seen in the next chapter), but in Gronert's case she received a lot of support. For example, the local spots union said in *Die Welt* in August 2007:

"We should support Sarah and stand by her in any way we can" said Ute Strakerjahn of the Westfälischen Tennis-Verband, the union that signed a declaration to support Sarah. At the time Sarah was in doubt whether she would end or continue her career the WTV said "she must be very strong and determined and we will do everything we can to help her."

Gronert and Semenya were both relatively young at that time, just 18 and 19. Both had a high testosterone level in the so-called male range. Ten nanomoles/L[4] was the cut-off for women in elite competition. Only testes produce these high levels of testosterone. Even with severe medical conditions of the adrenals or the ovaries a woman would never reach the cut-off without artificial help.

Semenya and Gronert both have a Y-chromosome and both have internal testes. Gronert doesn't react to male hormones, Semenya does. Sarah Gronert is a CAIS woman. Of course I don't know this for sure, we only know for sure that she is intersex. But she has no physical signs of a high T. Women with CAIS are overrepresented in sports. The major question is "why?"

I'm apt to think that her body-length-proportional long limbs are a factor that contributes to her success. In tennis, length matters. There is no need to explain this, because it's obvious. It's not a decisive factor in success, of course. Not every tall woman is a good tennis player. But if you've got talent and work hard, it's easier to reach your goals with some extra centimeters.

A genetic code for body length is found on the Y-chromosome. Men are typically taller than women. That goes for XY-women too. They are on average taller than XX-women. Body length matters in a great variety of sports, with the exception of sports like soccer and rugby. And body length most certainly matters in athletics like swimming and volleyball. But it's not considered unfair in competition, although the genetic instruction for length is on the Y-chromosome. Just as the SRY-chromosome. It would make more sense to look at a combination of physical traits in judging the eligibility of intersex athletes. Why?

If testosterone "closes the gap between XY-women and XX-women," why are there so many CAIS women on the playing fields? In 1996 eight (C) AIS women were initially suspended. That is far more than we might expect from the percentage of CAIS women in society. There must be an explanation for their sports success other than testosterone. Body length is one. Proportionally longer limbs can also play a role. Both are characteristics of CAIS. But neither are deemed unfair.

I am, however, still puzzled by the fact that Gronert had the most ferocious serves in the tour. "There is no girl who can hit serves like that, not even Venus Williams," said Schlomo Tzoref, the coach of Julia Glushko, whom Gronert beat in 2009 on her way to winning the 2009 Ra'anana tournament in Israel. "When I heard her story, I was in shock. I don't know if it's fair that she can compete or not. She does have an advantage, but if this is what the WTA has decided, they probably know best. If she begins to play continuously, within six months she will be within the Top 50," according to Intersexnews.blogspot.com. Her highest ranking was, however, 164.

For now will we stay on the tennis courts, not to discuss an intersex person but a transgender person who was suspended from the female tennis competition. And, strangely, after a gender verification. Through the story of Renée Richards I can clarify that the rules were more severe on intersex athletes than on the transgender ones, because the eligibility of transgender people in the female competition was regulated years before intersex athletes were, although the last category is biological and socially closer to XX-women.

In 2004 transgender women were eligible for the female competition after medical treatment. Another eight years passed before intersex athletes acquired the same regulation. The question that remains is: why are transgender people in elite sports more accepted than intersex athletes? Are transgender people better organized or is it fear of the biological unknown?

"They say I'm not a girl"

It's incomprehensible. Let's clarify this by the case of Renée—French for reborn—Richards.

Renée Richards was born Richard Raskind in the summer of 1934, in Forest Hills, Queens. Raskind's parents were medical specialists; Renée later became an eye surgeon herself. After trying out different sports at school he—he was a he at that time—chose to focus on tennis. After high school Richards attended Yale University and was captain of the men's tennis team. He graduated in 1959 from the University of Rochester Medical Center and specialized in ophthalmology. He played competitive tennis with a very effective left-handed serve.

During his college years Richards began dressing as a woman, which at the time was considered to be a perversion. In the 1950s dressing as a woman must have been quite a struggle for a young man. Richards visited several specialists in the fields of endocrinology, sexual reassignment and even a gynecological surgeon in Casablanca, Morocco. Richards by that time lived his life as a woman. He ultimately however decided against surgery, got married and fathered a son in 1972. The marriage ended three years later, in the year Richards finally resolved to undergo sex reassignment. He was 41 when he became a she. The transition was successful. Richards moved to California to work as an ophthalmologist in a joined practice. Richard was reborn as Renée.

Richards started competitive tennis again under a third name, Renée Clerck, but she was outed by a spectator who recognized the ferocious left-hand service of the former Richard Raskind. The U.S. tennis association then introduced the Barr Body Test to keep her out of competition. Richards refused to take the test. She was therefore excluded from all major championships, even Wimbledon. No test, no license.

But Richards took her case to a legal court. She sued the USTA in New York. The jurisdiction of the court was of course limited to the U.S. The Court of Arbitration for Sports was not founded until 1984; until then sports unions were free to make their own rules that were not hindered by national laws. To my knowledge Richards was the first athlete who took her case to court.

Richards accused the USTA of discrimination by gender in violation of the New York Human Rights Law. She asserted that participating in the tournament would constitute an acceptance of her right to be a woman.[5]

The U.S. Open Committee stated before the court: "There is competitive advantage for a male who has undergone a sex change surgery as a result of physical training and development as a male." That's an interesting argument. I'll be discussing this argument in the next chapter. The USTA was afraid that more male tennis players would choose to switch to the female competition. There never was, of course, a tsunami of transgender women (or disguised males) into the female competition.

In the meantime, Richards accepted the Barr Body Test and the result was ambiguous. She refused further testing and was banned from competition.

In August 1977, Judge Alfred M. Ascione ruled, "This person is now a female" and that requiring Richards to pass the Barr Body Test was "grossly unfair, discriminatory and inequitable, and a violation of her rights."[6] He also ruled that the USTA discriminated against Richards, and granted her an injunction against the USTA and the USOC, allowing her to play in the U.S. Open.

Richards lost to Virginia Wade in the first round of the singles competition, but made it to the finals in doubles. Richards played professional tennis until 1981. It wasn't always easy: In the Tennis Week Open in New Jersey 1976, 24 of the 31 competitors withdrew from the tournament because Richards would be playing there. They chose to play in a different tournament.

Although Richards won her legal case against the USTA, transgenderism remained controversial in elite sports. The IOC followed its own regulations, not being subjected to a U.S. court of law until 2004. In 2003, a committee convened by the IOC Medical Commission drew up new guidelines for participation of male athletes who had undergone sex reassignment. The report lists three conditions for participation. First, athletes must have undergone sex reassignment surgery, including changes in the external genitalia and a gonadectomy (removal of the testis). Second, athletes must show legal recognition of their gender. Third, athletes must have undergone hormone therapy for an appropriate time of at least two years before participation.

To me it's an enigma why these rules did not apply for intersex athletes as well, who were in this period and until 2010 barred for life from competition. They could have been welcomed in the sporting world under the same conditions as far as fair play was crucial for the new rules. But why weren't they allowed to participate sport if they followed the same conditions? Was it discrimination? That seems a fair moral judgment. So why were intersex athletes excluded from these new set of rules and did transgender people succeed?

"They say I'm not a girl"

Maybe it's because transgender people were (better) organized to stand up for their rights. Intersex people weren't organized at all. It was not until about 2016 that intersex people were joined to the LHBT community, making it LHBTI. Maybe the medical commission that proposed the new rules for transgender people forgot all about intersex athletes. Maybe the commission just didn't care as long as there was no organized protest. Was there a deep-rooted fear of the sexual unknown, maybe even of latent homosexuality? It's mysterious why the same rules were not applied for intersex athletes: gonadectomy and testosterone blockers. The intersex athletes already lived their lives officially as females. I'm not saying that you should introduce regulations for intersex athletes, on the contrary. I'm trying to understand why the intersex athletes in 2004 didn't get the same rights as transgender people. It was discrimination for sure.

Twelve years later, in 2016 male-to-female transgender athletes were allowed to compete without undergoing sex reassignment surgery, according to new guidelines adopted by the IOC.[7] The guidelines did not only apply for the Olympiads but the IOC also advised other sports organizations to adopt them. The guidelines were not restrictions but meant "to insure that trans athletes were not excluded from the opportunity to participate in sporting competition," the IOC said in a document on the website that outlines the guidelines. "The overriding sporting objective is and remains the guarantee of fair competition."[8]

So, for the male-to-female athletes the guidelines were by 2016 limited to hormone inhibiters and an official registration as female in the administration of their home country. One of the reasons for introducing the new guidelines was that in lots of modern countries gonadectomy was no longer legally required for transgender people to get registered officially as women. According to the IOC the new regulations were a human rights issue. Former IOC medical commission chairman Arne Ljungqvist said to the Associated Press: "We felt we cannot impose a surgery if that is no longer a legal requirement."[9]

The hormone therapy was aimed at a testosterone level below 10 nanomoles per liter in serum. That was the official cut-off for athletes, and it took at least one year of hormone therapy, but usually two years, to reach such a low level of testosterone in the bloodstream. The same testosterone level was required for hyperandrogen female athletes as of 2012. Females have on the average a testosterone level of 2 nanomoles/liter in serum. In males it can vary between 8 and 35 nanomoles.

So by 2016 the same rules applied for transgender women and hyper-androgen intersex athletes. Testosterone was considered to be the decisive factor that explained the gap between male and female athletes. At first glance this seems very logical, but in 2015 the Court of Arbitration for Sport concluded that there was not enough scientific evidence that intersex athletes profited from a high testosterone level. A 19-year-old Indian girl from West Bengal brought her case before the Court of Arbitration for Sports. With success!

That is probably because the effects of testosterone are the most societally shocking in a woman. For narrow hips we find no objection, and tall women may not be sexy according to some; what shocks us are the swollen muscle groups and facial hair. These attributes are seen as much more typically masculine than other biological factors. They are considered unwomanly. Apparently, androgen women do not fit with the image we have of women. And women are more and more willing to conform to that image. They are queuing at the depilation clinics.

The irony of the sex inspection is that the completely androgen-insensitive women are sometimes considered to be the sexiest women because of their lack of natural body hair and their perfect skin. It is therefore not surprising that they were the first to have unrestricted access to the competition. Of all women with a Y-chromosome, they are most in line with the classical Western ideal of female beauty.

Caster Semenya
and Dutee Chand
Changing the Rules

In 2009, Julius Malema of the South African ANC said, concerning Caster Semenya:

"Hermaphrodite," what is that? Somebody tell me, what is "hermaphrodite" in sePedi? There's no such thing, "hermaphrodite," in sePedi. So don't impose your hermaphrodite concepts on us. You are either a woman or a man. When a child is born you are announcing it's a baby girl or a baby boy. We have never heard in the village a child being projected: "We are given a hermaphrodite." In South Africa, in the villages, we only have boys and girls. A child is a boy or a girl. They can argue about this being determined scientifically, but in the villages we don't see signs, we don't have laboratories. When a child is born, we open its legs and that is the sign we use. The imperialists must not impose this on us if they have hermaphrodites where they come from. They must enjoy living with their hermaphrodites, because in South Africa there are no hermaphrodites. There's never been such a thing in the village we come from.[1]

He took the words right out of my mouth. From a certain point of view Malema is right, of course. Everybody is assigned a gender at birth. Pity he didn't know that in sePedi (one of the official languages of South Africa) a hermaphrodite is called a "setabane." I'm sure every language has a word for "hermaphrodite." But it's not a game of words, it's all about acceptance, although words can be denouncing too. But not by Malema. He was reacting to the argument about Caster Semenya, who was then a young girl from a village in Limpopo.

The South African 800-meter runner Caster Semenya and the Asian Indian sprinter Dutee Chand are both hyperandrogenic. Their T-level is high compared to other women. Chand and Semenya—in contrast to CAIS and AIS women—are sensitive to male hormones. Testosterone has effects on them, although their testosterone levels were low before they were born. That is why they have a DSD (disorder of sex development). The main question is of course whether they have an unfair advantage over other female athletes and therefore is it desirable to require them to get medical treatment. Apart from this the question remains if it is morally right to push healthy women into medical care.

Both runners were active without hormone treatment at the Rio Games in 2016, with varying degrees of success. Chand dropped out in the first heat, Semenya won the finals of the 800 handily. Both athletes were, willingly and unwillingly, responsible for a major change of course in the history of gender verification.

"Could This Women's World Champ Be a Man?" headlined *Time* magazine in 2009 after 18-year-old Caster Semenya became world champion at 800 meters in Berlin.[2] "The suspicion exists," wrote the reporter, "that she will lose her medal because she is actually a he." "She is a man" has been said many times about hyperandrogenic athletes. It is an illogical phrase. There is an inner contradiction, especially if you classify the sport competition as men's and women's. There is nothing wrong with that, but a she who is a he does not fit in any competition. And that is the consequence for women who are men, at least in the eyes of people who are ignorant of the question of intersexuality and for who there are only two categories, men and women. Journalists can also be unaware as can intersex athletes' competitors. The Italian Elisa Cusma said in 2009 about Semenya: "This kind of athlete should not run against us. She is not a woman, she is a man!" The teenage Semenya never said much about it herself, with the exception of a March 2018 article in *The Guardian*, in which she said:

> Since my victory in the female 800 meter event at the Berlin World Championships in August last year, I have been subjected to unwarranted and invasive scrutiny of the most intimate and private details of my being. Some of the occurrences leading up to and immediately following the Berlin World Championships have infringed on not only my rights as an athlete but also my fundamental and human rights, including my rights to dignity and privacy.[3]

In 2018 Sebastian Coe, chairman of the IAAF, stated that Semenya should be running with the men if she refused hormone treatment. He intended to re-introduce hormone therapy for hyperandrogenic women in the middle distance events, 400 meters to a mile. Not, as he said, because Semenya was a fraud, but because of a fair competition: "The IAAF has the responsibility to create a level playing field."[4] Instead of intensifying the battle against doping, he focused on the one woman who was different from the others. A woman who had committed no unfair sports crime. Between all athletes that benefit from genetic or biological characteristics—a seven-foot basketball player, a swimmer with Marfan Syndrome—he chose women with a natural high testosterone level. No human rights commission in the world would rule this as fair. But it turned out to be the story of Semenya's life.

It is important to note that Caster Semenya always strictly followed the rules of the IAAF and the IOC. After her first gender verification she was just 18 years old and the IAAF allowed her to start in spite of the regulations against intersex athletes. Before the Games of 2012 she took testosterone inhibiters in accordance with the new regulations for hyperandrogenic women. Instead of DNA testing, testosterone levels now determined the ability to enter the female competition. But in 2016 the Court of Arbitration for Sports had already suspended the new regulations for two years to give the IAAF more time to come up with a scientific answer to the question of whether a high level of natural testosterone gave an athlete an unfair benefit in the female competition. Still, Semenya's competitors were very hostile against her presence on the track. There's no excuse for their unsporting behavior. Semenya had every right to be there.

Over the last several years opinions and emotions have changed regarding Semenya. She has received more and more support, notably from Nelson Mandela. In September 2010, the British magazine *New Statesman* put Caster Semenya in their list of 50 people that matter.[5] According to the magazine, she "unintentionally revived the debate about gender, race and feminism and was thus an inspiration for gender campaigners worldwide." Semenya did indeed have a major influence on the way in which gender verification would proceed from now on, even though she was not personally involved in the deliberations.

In 2016, Semenya fully fulfilled her favorite role. She won the gold medal at the Rio Games with great ease and without hormone treatment. When she crossed the line, she made her usual muscle flexing gesture. It wasn't a very wise gesture, because she unconsciously made a connection between muscle strength and her victory. Between testosterone and performance. She rubbed salt in the wounds of the competition. Fortunately, she later skipped this small, unnecessary routine.

There was hardly any applause for her in Rio among some groups. This didn't seem to affect her. Nobody congratulated her, so she walked to the competitors herself and offered her hand to all of them. That was a moving gesture. After her silver medal in London 2012, Semenya finally had her gold medal and ultimately received the gold at the 2012 Olympics as well, because the initial winner, Maria Savinova, was disqualified as one of the Russian doping cases. In 2012 Semenya competed after mandatory hormone therapy, in 2016 she ran as herself. At both Games she took the gold, which might not be surprising because her high T had already done its job during puberty. "Testosterone in puberty and to a less extent also before puberty, has effects on growth and muscular strength and development. To exert its effect in further life continuous exposure to testosterone is needed. Testosterone has done some job in puberty, but is needed for increased muscular strength later on," wrote endocrinologist Birgit Kohler to me in an email on October 8, 2018. So yes, testosterone had already had some effect on growth and muscle strength.

During the championships after the games of 2016 Semenya won more and more respect from the audience. In England people were now cheering for her. But the dark clouds were again gathering above her head. Before we go there, let's first go back to her birth in 1991.

Semenya was born on January 7, 1991, as Mokgadi Caster Semenya in the village of Ga-Masehlong in South Africa. She grew up in Fairlie, deep in South Africa. The village is located in the northeast in the province of Limpopo. Ga-Masehlong is a village with mud huts and some stone houses. You can hardly find it on a map. The people are cheerful and friendly, even though there is nothing to do (according to modern concepts) and the facilities are scanty. Ga-Masehlong is proud of their Mokgadi. This also applies to the whole of South Africa, even though South African urbanites generally consider rural people contemptible.

Caster Semenya was named athlete of the year in 2016 in South Africa. That is very special for an intersexual athlete. It is unique that a country has so much respect for an athlete who got so little sympathy in the rest of the world. Outside South Africa, she is mostly considered an unfair competitor, even though she has always adhered to the rules. You cannot blame her at all. She is who she is. She does not doubt herself either. "God made me the way I am," she said in 2009 and she is satisfied with it.[6] "I am not fake. I do not want to be someone else. I do not want to be the person who wants to make others of me. I'm just me. I was born that way. I do not want any changes." She is right, you cannot demand someone to have medical interventions that are not necessary for their health. This doesn't necessarily mean that Semenya is not affected by the critiques of her. During the year she was not allowed to run, the year of the testosterone blockers, she got depressed.

The BBC wrote in 2009:

> A teenager too traumatized to take her university examinations. Her trainer Michael Semen told the South African newspaper *Beeld*: "Haar kop is baie moeg (Her head is very tired). Fortunately, the university has a good understanding of her situation and made it clear to her that exams are the last thing she should worry about at the moment," he said.

During this period Semenya was not allowed to speak on the subject.

The children in her native region play football. Semenya did too. She initially wanted to become a soccer player. The running she did served as good training for soccer. But she appeared to be a very talented middle-distance runner. In 2008 she won the 800 meters at the Commonwealth Youth Games with a time of 2:04.01. She was 17 years old. A year later she won the African Junior Championships and for the first time ran the 800 meters within 2 minutes: 1:56.72. It was almost eight seconds faster and the IAAF had its doubts about this very unusual progress. The International Athletics Federation required an investigation under the guise of a doping test. This turned out not to be on doping, it was a gender verification. Semenya didn't know this. She was not the only girl that had been brought under false pretenses to a sex test. I always wondered if the IAAF lied to protect the athlete or to protect themselves.

The news that Semenya underwent such an investigation leaked just before the finals of the 800 meters at the World Championships in Berlin in 2008. The leak led to many angry reactions, and the IAAF made every effort to defend itself. The federation admitted that there indeed had been a sex investigation, but that it had nothing to do with sexism or racism. The IAAF wanted to know whether Semenya unfairly benefited from a sex disorder. For the time being Semenya was still allowed to start in Berlin. That is unique in sports history. Without test results she was, according to the rules, still eligible. No verdict, no crime. Before the Semenya case athletes had to wait for test results. Semenya became world champion, running a time of 1:55.45. That was slower than the first world record in 1912 by the men, which was 1:51.9, and much slower than the current time of the best male runners; they were running 1:40.91. This is a head start of about 100 meters. There was no place for her in the male competition. Thus there was no alternative for Semenya.

The press got hold of the test result almost immediately. One of the experts involved in the IAAF's inspection leaked the results the *Sydney Daily Telegraph*.[7] "Caster Semenya is a hermaphrodite without uterus and ovaries." She has, the newspaper wrote, "internal testicles that produce testosterone." The anonymous source also told the newspaper that it was not Semenya's fault. She could not do anything about it. The IAAF did not deny the information but asked the press to treat her carefully: "We have received test results from the German doctors who have examined her and these results needed to be studied further. 'We will be discussing the results in private with the athlete in a few weeks' time.'"

South Africa was furious about the Australian publication of the test results. According to the South Africans the IAAF is sexist and racist, and thereby violating the human rights of their citizen. Nelson Mandela backed Semenya without reservation. The government of South Africa even filed a complaint at the United Nations,[8] claiming testing their compatriots was both sexist and racist. Semenya at this time seemed to simply shrug her shoulders. But was that an attitude or was she deeply hurt? The South African magazine *You* showed Semenya in pictures as very feminine, with her wearing dresses, make-up and jewelry. This attempt was not entirely successful, because Semenya never presented herself this way in daily life, being the kind of woman that looks better in shirt and trousers.

To make things worse, it turned out through leaked e-mails that the South African national association had already secretly investigated her in her own country. That is, before she went to Berlin. The teenager was not aware of the exact procedure and purpose of this medical examination. According to chairman Leonard Chuene, it was a doping test. On the basis of their medical examination the South African physicians advised the national federation to keep her in South Africa. Chuene ignored the advice. Word on the street was that Chuene first denied that he ordered a sex test, but later he did have to admit he was lying. The government of South Africa demanded the departure of Chuene.[9] Semenya's coach, Wilfried Daniels, also resigned because, as he himself said, he was unable to protect his pupil. It had become a human tragedy caused by headstrong sports powers. But apart from this traumatizing experience, it was finally clear to the IAAF that they could not go on like this. Something had to happen. Every few years the results of sex tests were on the streets and more and more protests by athletes were being upheld.

The *New Statesman* was right in 2010. Semenya was one of the 50 people that mattered in 2010. The IOC installed a medical committee to give advice on the admission of intersex women into competition. After eleven months this committee came to the conclusion that a high T-level gives a female athlete an unfair advantage. The hyperandrogenic athlete should bring her T-level down before being eligible. The committee wasn't troubled by scientific knowledge, as we shall see later on. After all, up to 2010 there wasn't any research done on the benefits of high endogenous (natural) androgens in sports. It's important to note at this point that there was no cut-off for the male competition.

Then Semenya disappeared off the radar. She decided to stay out of the spotlight and people respected her decision. In March 2010 she was not allowed to start in a competition in Stellenbosch. On July 6, 2010, Semenya got the green light from the IAAF. Her T-level must have dropped below the cut-off. It had been more than a year since the Berlin sex test. It must be noted that hormone treatments are not without risks—cardiac arrhythmias, nausea, thirst, excessive urination and mood swings are reported. There is no good reason in a medical sense for healthy women to impose such a cure. On the other hand, she could start again.

Semenya qualified for the Olympics in London 2012. Initially she won the silver medal in the 800 with a time of 1:57.23. This was almost 2 seconds slower than in Berlin, a decline of about 2 percent. This is a decline that matters on the 800 meters. But it's hard to say what caused it. Was it being out of training? Was it caused by fluctuations in her endocrine system? Was it the demoralizing effect of the sex tests and the publicity?

The rules changed drastically after 2012. From then on, women would no longer be suspended on the basis of a Y chromosome. But women whose testosterone level in the blood was above the cut-off of 10 nanomoles of testosterone per liter in serum—in short 10nm/L—first had to undergo a treatment of testosterone blockers and female hormones to bring the testosterone level below the cut-off (unless of course the athlete is CAIS). The average level in women is 2 or 3 nm/L.

The general opinion was that the new regulation signaled an end to the sex test. From then on just the T-level was going to be used. However, it still was a hidden sex test because biologic and genetic 46XY women could never reach the cut-off of 10nm/L, even with syndromes of the ovaries or adrenals.[10] So the regulations pertained to women with DSD. The cut-off didn't come out of the blue, it was meant for women with DSD.

In the opinion of the IAAF and the IOC T-levels above the cut-off are in violation of what the IAAF terms male and female range. The terminology is of course meant as an argument. But in reality the male range varies between 2 to 35 nanomoles of testosterone circulating naturally in their bodies. In fact, 16 percent of the male population has a testosterone level below 10 nanomoles. So if the cut-off is indeed a male range for the competition it would be reasonable that males with low T-levels would be allowed to take testosterone to reach the cut-off. But there is no such provision in the regulations for these male athletes.

But there was a bright spot too: suspending female athletes for life was over (unless an athlete refused hormone treatment, of course). That was a revolution in the history of gender testing. This committee of scientists worked for months on their advice, but apparently they failed to ask the most fundamental question: how can testosterone-insensitive women be so good at sports when there is no unfair benefit from their T-level? This should in my opinion be the central question. Because if we are able to define the beneficial factors of their success, we should be able to decide if the same factors apply to other hyperandrogenic athletes.

What makes the difference between male and female performance? Is it just testosterone? In response to the critics the IAAF wrote:

> The IAAF divides competition into male and female classifications because male athletes have clear performance advantages in terms of size, strength and power, as a result (in particular) of increased lean body mass and increased serum hemoglobin, which in turn is due mainly to the fact that, starting from puberty, they produce 10-30 times more testosterone than women. As noted above, the CAS has found that this difference justifies protecting female athletes from competition from male athletes.[11]

I'm not an endocrinologist but I doubt if body size is linked to testosterone. Body size is linked to genes on the sex chromosome. Men are usually taller than women. CAIS woman 46XY are on average taller than other 46XX women. They didn't grow taller through testosterone because they are insensitive to androgens. And size matters! Even in sports.

After installing the new rules the IAAF in 2013 brought four intersex women from rural areas in developing countries to a private clinic in France for treatment.[12] The IAAF paid all costs, requiring all concerned to keep this procedure secret. However, the physicians publicized the intervention in detail. Although no names were mentioned in the publication, the IAAF was outraged, especially by the fact that the surgeons mentioned that the women belonged to the same family. They suffered from a rare genetic disorder. According to the IAAF it would be quite easy to find out the names of the athletes. And this proved once again how hard it is to keep things secret. What had happened in the private clinic?

Undescended testes were taken out, to enable the athletes to test below the cut-off and resume competing. The women had given their permission for this intervention, called gonadectomy. This surgery was, however, medically redundant. After all, all four women were healthy women. And gonadectomy is irreversible. So, with this operation, the four young women made the final decision how to continue their lives.

Why did the IAAF prefer gonadectomy to a simpler hormone cure? Even the anti-conception pill would have been sufficient to bring the testosterone level of the women below the cut-off of 10 nm/L. In her dissertation, Yvette Zimmerman showed that the so-called combination pill lowers the testosterone level 60 to 80 percent.[13] The anti-conception pill would have been sufficient as treatment. The IAAF made one mistake after another in their drive for a level playing field.

And then again, can women from developing countries truly make free decisions, if there's a lot of sponsorship money at stake? If they feel obliged to feed their family members? This is, of course, a rhetorical question. These secret operations are against everything that sports stands for. Even if the athletes approved. You just cannot operate on healthy sports women. And most certainly not if the women are not allowed to take hormone treatment to bring their level to the average level of women. Missing ovaries, the treated women have a very low level of testosterone after the medical intervention because ovaries also produce testosterone. It would be quite fair to give these treated athletes permission to complement their androgen level to normal female values (2 nanomoles). But even athletes with very low T-levels are not allowed to use synthetic testosterone.

Semenya complied with the rules and brought her T-level below the cut-off with medication. But just a few years after the testosterone regulations were introduced, the Court of Arbitration for Sport suspended them, thanks to the brave 19-year-old Dutee Chand, who brought her case before the court. That is why Semenya could participate in the Rio Games the way she was, with her normal level of endogenous testosterone.

Dutee Chand grew up—where else?—in a rural village, Gopalpur, in the east of India. Her house was a hut without electricity and running water. Her parents were illiterate weavers who earned eight dollars a week. Dutee and her six siblings were all destined for the same fate: weaving in a five-by-two hut. But Dutee had other plans. She found she had a talent for sprinting.

Dutee was born on February 3, 1996, in the Indian village of Odisha. She started competing in 2007 in the junior-level competition. By 2019 she was the Indian champion in the 100 meters sprint. She followed her ten-year-older sister Saraswati literally in her footsteps. At the age of four, she was already dribbling with her sister and later ran barefooted with her sister along the Brahmani River. She had a lot more talent for sprinting than her sister, although you might not expect a world-class sprinter to come from India, because they lack the ACTN3 gene, the sprint gene.

Dutee's parents asked her to give up athletics and learn to weave, but Saraswati managed to convince them that Dutee could earn more as an athlete than as a weaver. The district government was convinced of Dutee's talent and from early on provided a daily meal package for the family: meat, vegetables and eggs. That was policy for all talented athletes in the district. Because Saraswati also brought in money that she had been winning in the marathon circuit, Dutee was allowed to run. Saraswati measured Dutee's feet with a piece of string and traveled by bus for about four hours to buy her some running shoes, along with a track suit. In 2006, Dutee, at 10 years old, got an accommodation in the Indian training facility National Institute of Sports (NIS). Dutee Chand had no idea then that her fate would be the same as Santhi Soundarajan, who was barred in that year.

Just like every other intersex athlete, Dutee doesn't get periods. Her mother had reassured her that that time would come for her. At the age of 16 she was junior champion of India in the 100 meters at 11.8 seconds. That was also the time of the golden record of Stella Walsh in 1933, but slower than Helen Stephens in 1936. In 2018 Chand clocks her fastest sprint at 11.24. That's 0.01 slower than Ewa Klobukowska in 1965. We would never have known her name if she wasn't sex tested. But then again, she still was the fastest sprinter in India. Interesting to note is that in 2018 the fastest woman sprinter would be number 3,426 on a unisex ranking list.

In June 2014 Chand qualified for the Commonwealth Games, but the Indian Athletics Union dropped her at the last minute. Shortly after that, Chand was cooling down after a 200-meter race when the phone rang. It was the chairman of the Indian Athletics Union AFI who asked her to come to Delhi. She undertook a five-hour bus ride and upon arrival was immediately sent to a clinic where she met a doctor from the IAAF. He told her that he would do the normal blood and urine tests. And there would be an ultrasound to investigate where her abdominal complaints come from. Dutee could not remember having abdominal complaints. The doctor assured her that all was routine. What Chand did not know at the time was that she was considered suspicious by the officials and by the competition. They found her too muscular. And her steps were also very strong for a small girl 1 meter 60 cm (5 feet 3 inches) in height.

Three days after the ultrasound, the federation sent a letter titled, "Subject: Gender Verification Issue" to the Indian government's sports authority.

> It has been brought to the notice of the undersigned that there are definite doubts regarding the gender of an athlete Ms Dutee Chand. The athlete has won a Gold Medal in 200m (Women) and as well as 4 × 400 Relay (Women), in the recently concluded 17th Asian Junior Athletics Championships held at Chinese Taipei. During the above mentioned championships, also, doubts were expressed by the Asian Athletics Association regarding her gender issue.
>
> As is aware [sic] that in the previous past also such cases of female hyper androgenism[14] have brought embarrassment to the fair name of sports in India.
>
> In view of the above you may like to conduct gender verification test of Ms. Dutee Chand as per the established protocol, so as to avoid any embarrassment to India in the international arena at a later stage. The matter may be taken up on an urgent basis as the athlete is bound to leave on 18th July 2014, for World Junior Athletics Championships.

The federation should have said that the hyperandrogenic Chand had a presumed unfair benefit. But instead, the sports union was afraid that she would cause embarrassment to India. How could she cause embarrassment by winning medals for India? Since when did sports unions protect the image of a nation?

The *Sydney Morning Herald* reported:

> Shortly after, she was sent to a private hospital in Bangalore, where a curt woman drew her blood to measure her level of natural testosterone, though Chand had no idea what was being measured. Chand also underwent a chromosome analysis, an MRI and a gynecological exam that she found mortifying. To evaluate the effects of high testosterone, the international athletic association's protocol involves measuring and palpating the clitoris, vagina and labia, as well as evaluating breast size and pubic hair scored on an illustrated five-grade scale.[15]

The endocrinologists told the IFA that her male hormone levels were too high. The levels were not made public but must, of course, have been above the 10 nanomoles threshold for the female competition. The IFA told her that she was not allowed to run for a year, and that her T-value should be reduced in that year. She also received this judgment by mail: "You are suspended for the time being from every athletic competition with immediate effect." She lost her place in the national team. Chand was flabbergasted; she had never heard of the term testosterone, let alone nanomoles per liter.

Chand was absolutely distraught when the press called her, asking enigmatic questions about the androgen test. She had no idea what the press was asking about. It wasn't that she was not clever, but she had never heard about such concepts. The journalist wanted to know if there had been a gender test. She asked him, "What is a gender test?" In any case, the press obviously knew about her situation. At first, Chand was not aware of the severity of her condition and her position. But as things become clearer to her she was deeply shocked. "I cried for three straight days after reading what people were saying about me," she said, regarding what she saw being debated on internet forums. "They were saying, 'Dutee: Boy or girl?' and I thought, how can you say those things? I have always been a girl."[16] This was a painful episode in Chand's life.

In the news they said that I was a boy, someone else said that I was transsexual. I am a person, but I felt like an animal. How can I continue with so much humiliation? I feel it is wrong to change your body for sport participation. I'm not changing for anyone. It is like in some societies where they used to cut off the hand of people caught stealing. I feel like this is the same kind of primitive, unethical rule. It goes too far.

"They have tested her at the last minute, humiliated her and broken her heart," *The Hindu* reported that same month. "All sorts of things have been written about her. Now, if she re-enters the sports field, things will not be normal. Even if she takes treatment, people will kill her with their suspicious gaze."

Santhi Soundarajan felt the matter could have been dealt with discreetly. "That things became public, is wrong. Would they have done it if it was their daughter?" she asked. "Who is responsible for her future now? The job and the money are secondary problems. Think about how much she would have suffered. She is not from a wealthy or powerful family; just another ordinary family."[17]

The moment lawyers and sports experts heard that Chand was suspended, she was offered assistance. Especially from Dr. Payoshni Mitra, an activist film director with a doctorate in gender studies and who was once a tomboy playing badminton. Mitra encouraged Chand to fight back. She offered her help with composing a letter directed to the Athletics Federation in India (the AFI). In her letter Chand stated, among other things, that

> my testosterone level is natural and that I have not used doping. I am obliged to undergo medical treatment for which according to experts the basis is unscientific. The treatment is also irreversible and will be able to damage my health now and in the future. The treatment has serious side effects. I do not understand why I have to undergo this treatment to be admitted to the female competition. I was born as a woman and grew up as a woman. I request you to allow me to take part in the national competition without medical treatment. I have trained half my life to get to where I am now and to make sure that my country is proud of me.

She concluded, "Please allow me to play sports. Should you suspend me for the time being, I will turn to the Court of Arbitration for Sport."

Payoshni Mitra encouraged Chand to present her case to the Court of Arbitration for Sport in Switzerland. So, no half measures would be taken. In short, the case centered around "the validity of the IAAF regulations governing the eligibility of females with hyperandrogenism to compete in the female competition."[18] Mitra and Chand had several arguments.

First and foremost: there was no scientific proof that naturally occurring testosterone significantly contributes to performance on the track. In other words, Chand does not benefit from her testosterone level.

Second, the testosterone rule is discriminatory because the rule only applies for women. According to Mitra you have to treat men and women equally in accordance with the charter of the IOC (and of course not only according to the IOC).

In March 2015, the case came before three judges and the testimonies of sixteen experts were heard for four days. Two American lawyers represented Chand in Lausanne. She was only 19 years old. Mitra acted as her mediator. The CAS, led by the Australian judge Annabelle Clair Bennet, took her complaint very seriously. Among the sixteen witnesses were doctors, ethicists, a sports director and athletes. Two issues were important; first, whether the rules were discriminatory, and second, whether there was sufficient scientific evidence that the body's own testosterone significantly improved performance.

The issues that arose for determination by the CAS panel in this case may be summarized as follows:

1. Do the hyperandrogenism regulations discriminate impermissibly against certain female athletes on the basis of : (i) a natural physical characteristic; and/or (ii) sex?

2. Should the hyperandrogenism regulations be declared invalid on the basis that there is insufficient scientific evidence: (i) that endogenous testosterone improves athletic performance in female athletes; and/or (ii) that 10 nmol/L is the scientifically correct threshold at which female athletes are in the "male range" of endogenous testosterone and therefore enjoy the benefits of male levels of androgens?

3. Are the hyperandrogenism regulations disproportionate in the context of: (i) the fact they discriminate on the basis of a natural physical characteristic and/or sex; and/or (ii) the harm they cause to female athletes?

4. Are the hyperandrogenism regulations invalid because they are a form of unauthorized antidoping sanction in violation of Articles 4.3.3, 10 and 23.2.2 of the World Antidoping Agency Code?

The first issue of discrimination was quickly dealt with. The IAAF admitted that women and men are treated differently by the hyperandrogenism regulations. Male athletes with an excessive high T-value are not obliged to undergo any hormone treatment. According to the IAAF, this discrimination is necessary in order to give hyperandrogenic women access to the competition. The court, however, agreed with Chand: It was discriminatory and the IAAF should therefore take measures.

The second issue was the scientific basis for the regulations. Does testosterone improve the performance of female athletes and to what extent? This was, of course, the central question of the trial. Is there enough evidence that hyperandrogenic woman benefit from a high T-level? The IAAF stated that hyperandrogenic women have a competitive advantage provided by their elevated testosterone levels and that medical science should bring these values down. However, Chand's lawyers argued that there is no scientific basis for this argument and that the regulations should therefore be annulled. An important argument from the Chand lawyers is that androgen-insensitive women are disproportionally represented in elite competition (in regard to the general population) and therefore apparently perform very well without testosterone. What makes these athletes so good? Is it body length, bone density or maybe lean body mass? That was obviously a very important argument, as I've written before.

According to the IAAF it has been scientifically proven that testosterone is the most effective factor in sports performance for men. British professor of endocrinology Richard Holt, however, indicated that the testosterone rule is inadequate for women. He quoted from a study by Healy et al. that showed that the lean body mass of women is on average 10 kilos lower and that this factor explains the differences in sports performances between men and women (the LBM is the weight without fat). According to him there was no connection between the testosterone level and the lean body mass. He further disputed the assumption that there is a female and male range in testosterone. There was more an overlapping level. Holt pointed out the other biological factors discussed here that determine performance differences, such as body height. According to Holt, all top athletes are outliers. Holt presented many endocrinologic arguments, including the most important: that synthetic and body hormones have different effects on the otherwise very complex hormonal system. You cannot compare the effect of synthetic testosterone with endogenous testosterone. The chemical composition is different.

The scientific experts of the IAAF stated that Holt had misinterpreted the scientific articles. Moreover, the expert witness of the IAAF stated that the hyperandrogenic women who had undergone treatment performed worse after the medical intervention. The opponents did not dispute this, but estimated that the better performance of women with a high T-value was no more than three percent, according to unpublished research. The treatment was therefore disproportional.

Of course, Chand's lawyers pointed out that the testosterone measure causes disproportionate damage to the self-confidence and gender identity of intersex athletes. That sportswomen had been stigmatized and that the results of research had been leaked to the press too often. The IAAF defended itself by declaring that it was hardly to blame and that it was in the great majority without breach of privacy. The discussion that took place was very complete and during the process was minutely documented in 160 pages in the CAS report. The verdict is available online. Readers who want to know all the details of this discussion may want to read this interim arbitral award, available on the web. The CAS judges decided that the scientific basis for the testosterone regulations was not convincing. The IAAF had to do their homework again.

What about the competition? What did the athletes say about it? Interestingly, after their careers were over, some athletes had adjusted their opinion by 180 degrees. Like Maria Martinez Patiño, who herself was a victim of gender verification but later cleared. She surprisingly stood up as a proponent of the testosterone regulations, provided that the preconditions would improve. The privacy of the athletes should be better protected. Martinez Patiño stated that she once opposed the rules, but since she became an advisor to the IOC she had adjusted her opinion. This proves the adage that he who pays the piper calls the tune. Time, she said, had taught her that the rules were fair. According to her, the pain was not in the research itself, but in the question of whether or not you were a woman.

But there was also another voice from the competition. Special was the testimony of 880-meter runner Madeleine Pape, who was defeated by Caster Semenya in her last big game before her suspension. "In those days," Pape testified, "I agreed with women who said that Caster Semenya did not belong in the competition." But in 2012, the brand-new sociologist Pape started her dissertation about women in sports. "When I finished my career, I learned to think more critically about these issues. I did not know that there was so much moral opposition to gender verifications." Education is, like Mandela said, the most powerful weapon to change the world.

The CAS suspended the regulations for a period of two years. The IAAF had not made it sufficiently clear that the regulations were necessary and proportionate to achieve a fair competition. According to the judges, the IAAF had not made it clear that there was a scientifically demonstrable relationship between a high T level and sports performance in hyperandrogenic women. The panel therefore wanted to know whether a person's own testosterone could contribute to their performance and in what percentages.

Dutee Chand was overjoyed with the preliminary result "not only for me, but for all women like me." She had gone through a dark period in her life and faced the challenge with courage. She could now look ahead with hope. Her coach, Ramesh, praised her courage. "It was a long fight," he said, "but I knew we would win. Dutee is special. All other athletes would already have given up if they had to experience what she has experienced." I'm sure he was right. This required so much courage and perseverance from a 19-year-old woman.

Maria Martinez Patiño found the decision of the three judges of the CAS "a mistake, but a good mistake. We are going to learn from this mistake in Rio." Rio would become the testing ground for this issue, because now Chand and Semenya would participate as they were made, without any treatment. Martinez Patiño was firmly convinced she was right; hyperandrogenic women would win with preponderance. Semenya did, Chand did not.

After months of deliberation, the IOC decided to suspend the hyperandrogen regulations until the CAS could come to a verdict, planned for July 2017. So Chand and Semenya and other hyperandrogen women could participate in the 2016 Games in Rio without medical treatment. Employees and consultants at the IOC were shocked by the preliminary CAS ruling. Most of the anger came from transgender athletes. Transgender woman Joanna Harper, advisor of the IOC, was the most outspoken. Her carefully built construction threatened to collapse. Surgery was no longer required, as long as man-to-woman transgender athletes followed a hormone treatment with testosterone blockers. Transgender people just had to bring their T-level down. The fear of was that the IOC would put surgery back into the regulations. That would be fundamentally wrong, according to Harper. I do not want to judge on this standpoint, but it can be easily guessed that female athletes would refuse to run against biological men with high T-levels. It would mean the end of a separate competition for men and women. It's useful to say at this point that some scientists pleaded for a competition where athletes were no longer separated by gender but classified by testosterone level. This would mean that men with very low T-levels would be competing against women, and athletes like Semenya would be running in a largely male group. But of course this would cause new problems and challenges for sports unions and athletes.

Discussions about the testosterone regulations and the question of whether these regulations were supported by science were also taking place outside the CAS. *The Journal of the American Medical Association* stated during this period that there is no essential difference between a congenital syndrome that leads to higher testosterone production and, for example, a genetic mutation that gives high hemoglobin values, in short, a better transport of oxygen in the blood. As an example, the scientific journal mentioned the former cross-country skier Eero Mantyranta whose hemoglobin level is 50 percent higher than the average. In both cases, these are congenital syndromes that can benefit an athlete. Why one must be treated and the other does not remained unclear, according to the journal.

Semenya won the gold in Rio with force majeure. There were also doubts, apparently, about the athletes who came in second and third, Margaret Wambui from Kenya and Francine Niyonsaba from Burundi.

"Everyone can see it's two separate races, so there's nothing I can do," Lynsey Sharp of Scotland said, in tears after the race.[19] After the finish she aligned with Melissa Bishop and Joanna Jozwik, possibly to indicate that the three of them ran a "pure race." Sharp claimed after the game that there were actually "two separate races"; theirs and those of the African runners. But in London 2012 Sharp also lost to Semenya and Niyonsaba. Semenya was invincible in the 800 meters in Rio, but did this mean that she cannot be beaten? Her best time was not yet matching the top ten best 800-meter runners. It's just that in 2016 there was no better runner in the competition.

Dutee Chand flew to Rio de Janeiro on August 5, a tiring flight of 30 hours. The team management flew business class, the athletes economy class—a rather bizarre relationship, about which she rightly complained in the newspaper. It reminds one of the 1920s in the Netherlands when the head honchos got a good hotel bed and skaters like Siem Heiden in St. Moritz had to sleep in the bathroom. That is, almost 100 years later, apparently still the case in India. How do you as a country win medals if you deal with your athletes like that? Chand said after the heats that she had suffered from the journey and the time difference. You should indeed prepare yourself much better for such an important event.

Chand got stuck in the heats. She became 50th in a field of 69 women, with a disappointing time of 11.69. However, she was not dissatisfied herself. For the first time in 36 years there was an Indian sprinter at the Olympic Games. She was happy to represent her country and meet the big runners like Usain Bolt and Elaine Thompson. And she was only 20, so in four years she would still be strong enough. Unfortunately, no one welcomed her back to India after the Games. That would of course have done her good. Maybe we will see her back in Tokyo, with or without hormone treatment. She is, in any case, a big name in athletics thanks to her courage to stand up against discrimination and exclusion in sport.

The "testing ground Rio" therefore provided an ambiguous answer. Testosterone is not a panacea. Testosterone does not necessarily yield gold. The matter is not that simple. Winning is hard work, being motivated, having talent, the right genes and nature certainly also helps: organic factors are often decisive. Testosterone is not a ticket for gold. But it is deemed as unfair. But sports are never really fair. I have never—for instance—heard anyone complain about the relatively long limbs and big hands of Michael Phelps. These are symptoms of Marfan Syndrome. One might argue that his participation was unfair. You couldn't beat him no matter how hard you were training. No matter how talented you were. He was invincible; intersex athletes are not.

In 2017 the IAAF published a scientific article just in time for the verdict of the CAS. The CAS postponed the verdict again for half a year in order to study this publication. The object of the study: "To test the influence of serum androgen levels on performance, male and female athletes were classified in tertiles according to their free testosterone (fT) concentration and the best competition results achieved in the highest and lowest fT tertiles were then compared."

Looking at the levels of free testosterone was the right thing to do. Free testosterone is not bound to certain enzymes, it is the testosterone an athlete is free to use. Testosterone has, after all, different functions in the human body; one of them is the sex drive. These parts of the hormone substance are "earmarked" for a specific function. Bone strength, brain functions and muscle mass are also earmarked functions. Free testosterone is measured in micromoles. A micromole is one millionth of a mole. So we are speaking of very, very small amounts.

The conclusion of the research by Dr. Stéphane Bermon et al. is that "female athletes with high fT levels have a significant competitive advantage of 1.8–4.5% over those with low fT in 400 m, 400 m hurdles, 800 m, hammer throw, and pole vault."[20] Hyperandrogenic athletes should thereby, according to the IAAF, bring their elevated T-level down to less than 5 nanomoles/L. So the cut-off should become 5 nm/L instead of 10.

The first conclusion that could be made through this research is that Chand won her case against the IAAF. Testosterone levels have no significant competitive advantage on the 100-meter sprint. That was the good news for Chand, but the bad news was of course for Caster Semenya. The IAAF planned new testosterone regulations for the middle distances by November 2018. Semenya should lower her testosterone level to be able to compete in the 800 meters, bringing it below the new strict cut-off of 5 nanomoles per liter in serum.

If she refused, "she should be competing with the men," as IAAF chairman Sebastian Coe remarked.[21] This goes to show that he has no idea about the sensitivity of the subject. Gender is not something you can change overnight. Let alone that she would finish well behind the best male 800-meter runners. Coe said about the new rules: "This is not about cheating. No hyperandrogenic athlete has cheated. This is about our responsibility as a sport federation to ensure a level playing field. It is for us to decide the rules, to draw the lines for competition."

The IAAF published the new rule on April 28 on their website. The new regulations require any athlete who has a Difference of Sexual Development (DSD) that results in her levels of circulating testosterone being five nmol/L in serum or above, and who is androgen-sensitive, to meet certain criteria to be eligible to compete in "restricted events" in international competition (or to set a world record at a competition that is not an international competition):

(a) she must be recognized by law either as female or as intersex (or equivalent);
(b) she must reduce her blood testosterone level to below 5 nmol/L for a continuous period of at least six months (e.g., by use of hormonal contraceptives); and
(c) thereafter she must maintain her blood testosterone level below 5 nmol/L continuously (i.e., whether she is in competition or out of competition) for so long as she wishes to remain eligible.

The first interesting fact is that the regulation is aimed at women with a DSD. So a woman with another syndrome that leads to a high T-level does not have to bring her level below five nanomoles. Thus, this is not about fairness; this is about gender.

The second interesting fact is that the federation introduced a stricter maximum T-level than previously. It is now five instead of ten nanomoles/L, which was the rule of the IOC in 2010. The obvious target is Semenya, because it would be fairly easy to bring her level down to less than 10 nanomoles.

According to the *Sydney Morning Herald,* which published the outcomes of the 2008 sex verification, Semenya has three times the usual level for a woman. That would be just a little bit less or more than 10 nm/L, the average level being 2 to 3 nm/L. No wonder journalists and politicians commented on the rules as being sexist and as well as calling out the blatant racism.[22]

In the week the new study of the IAAF was published, three researchers found serious problems when they performed a partial replication of the IAAF study. Pielke, Tucker and Boye did the replication because, as they state, "the IAAF publication has serious consequences for female athletes in the competition." They called for a retraction of the publication because of serious faults in the data. "They cannot use this study as an excuse or a reason for setting a testosterone level because the data they have presented is not solid," one of the independent researchers, Erik Boye of Norway, said.[23]

The disputed 2017 study in the journal examined results from the 2011 and 2013 world track and field championships. It found that women with the highest testosterone levels significantly outperformed women with the lowest testosterone levels in events such as the 400 meters, the 400-meter hurdles and the 800 meters, which distill speed and endurance.

But in examining the study's results from those three races, plus the 1,500 meters, the three independent researchers said they found that the performance data used in the study's analysis was anomalous or inaccurate 17 percent to 33 percent of the time. The errors included more than one time recorded for the same athlete; repeated use of the same time for individual athletes; and phantom times when no athlete could be found to have run a reported time. Also included were times for athletes who were disqualified for doping.

"I think everyone can understand that if your data set is contaminated by as much as one-third bad data, it's kind of a garbage-in, garbage-out situation," said one of the independent researchers, Roger Pielke, Jr., the director of the Sports Governance Center at the University of Colorado.

Referring to the IAAF, Pielke said, "I really see no option for them other than to retract the paper. If they retract the paper, then the regulations don't have a scientific basis."

Pielke concluded that in the publication there were 220 errors in performance data of the athletes. The IAAF updated the publication but did not intend to withdraw it. Bernon, co-author of the IAAF study and scientific consultant to the athletic union, admitted the faults but wrote in an email to one of the independent researchers that the 220 faults "do not have significant impact on the final outcomes and conclusions of our study." The IAAF was of course not amused but held on to the new regulation.

Caster Semenya objected to the rule, said she would fight the decision and called it unlawful. "It is not fair. I just want to run naturally, the way I was born."[24] The IAAF agreed to honor a decision.

Gender verification should stop. It's humiliating and unnecessary. There never was a valid argument for this procedure. Sex tests have ruined the lives of many women. Far too many. This is mostly because gender verification is far too delicate an issue to be left to sports federations. No matter how hard they try, every time there is an anomalous result they seem to violate athletes' privacy. Fair play is an illusion. There would only be fair play if every athlete with a certain physical benefit was barred. If that were the case, sport would be dull to watch indeed.

Chapter Notes

Preface

1. Dohle, Max. "Het verwoeste leven van Foekje Dillema: de grootste tragedie uit de Nederlandse sportgeschiedenis," *Arbeiderspers* (Amsterdam), 2008.
2. Stéphane Bermon and P. Garnier, "Serum Androgen Levels and Their Relation to Performance in Track and Field: Mass Spectrometry Results from 2127 Observations in Male and Female Elite Athletes." *British Journal of Sports Medicine* (September 5, 2017): 1309–1314; Interim Arbitral Award: Dutee Chand vs Athletics Federation of India and the International Association of Athletics Federations. Numbered 205. Court of Arbitration for Sport, Lausanne, 2015.
3. "How Common Is Intersex?," Intersex Society of North America, www.isna.org.
4. Mayabhushan Nagvenkar, "Goa's Pinki Praminik," Newslaundry.com, July 21, 2012.
5. Bermon, 2017.

Preliminaries

1. "Witold Smętek," wikipedia.org.
2. Mededeling Nederlandsch Tijdschrift voor Geneeskunde, 1936.
3. Vanessa Heggie. "The H Word: Sex Testing and the Olympics: Myths, Rumours and Confirmation Bias," guardian.com, August 2, 2012.
4. Clare Tebbutt, "The Spectre of the 'Man-Woman Athlete': Mark Weston, Zdenek Koubek, the 1936 Olympics and the Uncertainty of Sex," *Woman's History Review*, 24.5 (2015): 721–738.
5. J. Hargreaves and E. Anderson, *Routledge International Handbook of Sport, Gender and Sexuality* (Routledge, 2014).
6. Tebbut, "The Spectre."
7. Cyd Zeigler, "18 Out LGBT Participants in the Women's World Cup," Outsports.com, May 31, 2015.
8. "History for All: The History of Women's Football," TheFA.com, undated.
9. Susan Cahn, *Coming On Strong: Gender and Sexuality in 20th-Century Women's Sports* (Cambridge: Harvard University Press, 1995).
10. "Alice Milliat," Wikipedia.
11. "Het bizarre leven van Violette Morris: autocoureur, travestiet en nazibeul," *Het Nieuwsblad*, January 11, 2017. See also Anne Sebba, *Les Parisiennes: How the Women of Paris Lived, Loved and Died under Nazi Occupation* (St. Martin's Press, 2016).
12. "Dokument Ramm: Erkjennelsen," https://youtu.be/ehnMEjHyIgM.
13. "Homosexuality in Association Football," Wikipedia.
14. Oliver Brown, "The Person

Who Pays for Everything Is the Athlete," telegraph.co.uk, November 14, 2016.

15. M. Genel, "Gender Verification No More?" *Medscape Women's Health* (May-June 2000), pubmed.org.

16. Frans Klumper, personal interview, September 21, 2016.

17. See the biographies in the last chapter of this book. They are about girls from rural communities in India and South Africa.

18. K. Koman, *Een koningin met mannenbenen: Fanny Blankers-Koen atlete van de eeuw* (Amsterdam: Dedico Grave, 2003).

19. Leni Riefenstahl, *Olympia Fest der Völker* (Berlin, 1938).

20. Guy Walters, *Berlin 1936: How Hitler Stole the Olympian Dream* (London, 2006).

21. Gabriela Szabo, "True Romania," Surprisingromania.blogspot.com.

22. John Bosley Ziegler, NIDA Research Monograph Index, Wikipedia, 1990.

23. Gina Kolata, "I.O.C. Panel Calls for Treatment in Sex Ambiguity Cases," *New York Times*, January 20, 2010.

24. Rob Velthuis, "Is Semenya vrouw genoeg om aan de Spelen me te mogen doen?" *Dagblad Trouw & Nieuwsblad,* August 18, 2016.

25. Denise Lewis, "Semenya Will Top the Podium—Yet She Can Never Win," *Telegraph*, August 16, 2016.

26. "Medicine. Change of Sex," *Time* magazine, August 24, 1936.

27. "Girl Changes into Man," *Your Body*, August 1936.

28. Tebbut, "The Spectre."

29. Article in *Time* magazine (April 1936), in Tebbut, "The Spectre."

30. "Het mysterie Foekje Dillema," Andere Tijden Sport VPRO Hilversum, July 8, 2008.

31. Tebbut, "The Spectre."

32. Tebbut, "The Spectre."

33. Tebbut, "The Spectre."

34. Tebbut, "The Spectre."

The XX-Games

1. Stephane Bermon et al., "Women with Hyperandrogism in Elite Sports: Scientific and Ethical Rationales for Regulating," *The Journal of Clinical Endocrinology and Metabolism,* vol. 100, issue 3 (March 2015). Academic.oup.com.

2. Announcement in the Nederlands Tijdschrift voor Geneeskunde, September 1936.

3. Vanessa Heggie, "Testing Sex and Gender in Sports: Reinventing, Reimagining and Reconstructing Histories," *Endeavour* 34, 4 (December 2010): 157–163.

4. *Sport Olympic Games.* Brundage wanted "to make sure that athletes were really 100% female." *Time*, August 10, 1936.

5. Tebbut, "The Spectre."

6. Allen Guttman, The Olympics: A History of the Modern Games (Google Books, 1992).

7. Dohle, "Het verwoeste."

8. "World Games Athletics," Wikipedia.

9. "IAAF Introduces New Eligibility Regulations for Female Classification," 2018, www.iaaf.org.

10. "Gender Verification in Sports," Wikipedia.

11. The IAAF suspended Santhi Soundarajan, Dutee Chand and Caster Semenya.

12. Dohle, "Het verwoeste."

13. "So What If Some Olympian Females Have High Levels of Testosterone?" theconversation.com, August 15, 2016.

14. Ibid.

15. The case of Carla de Vries in this book clarifies this. She was not informed.

16. Yvonne van Gennip, personal interview, November 2010.

17. Dohle, "Het verwoeste."

18. Sylvia Cheeseman, personal interview, March 2008.

19. Los Angeles Times, August 13, 1970.

20. Fady Hannah-Shmouni et al., "Revisiting the Prevalence of Nonclassic Congenital Adrenal Hyperplasia in U.S. Ashkenazi Jews and Caucasians," Genetics in Medicine (November 19, 2017), Pubmed.com.

21. Bruce Kidd and Cesar Torres, Historicizing the Pan-American Games (Routledge, 2015), no page number.

22. Ibid.

23. Jaime Schultz, Qualifying Times: Points of Change in U.S. Women Sport (Urbana: University of Illinois Press, 2014).

24. L. Elias, A. Ljungqvist, M. Ferguson-Smith et al., "Gender Verification of Female Athletes," Genetics in Medicine (2000): 249–254; Dohle, "Het verwoeste."

25. Ruth Padawer, "The Humiliating Practice of Sex Testing Female Athletes," New York Times Magazine, June 28, 2016.

26. P.A. Jacobs and J.A. Strong, "A Case of Human Intersexuality Having a Possible XXY Sex-Determining Mechanism," January 31, 1959, Pubmed.com.

27. "Is Athletic Performance Determined by Genetics?" U.S. National Library of Genetics, undated, ghr.nlm.nih.gov.

28. L. Elias, A. Ljungqvist, M. Ferguson-Smith, et al., "Gender Verification of Female Athletes," Genet Med (July-August 2002), www.ncbi.nlm.nih.gov.

29. Robert Ritchie et al., "Intersex and the Olympic Games," Journal of the Royal Society of Medicine (August 1, 2008).

30. Heere Aad, personal interview, May 2007.

31. Elias et al., "Gender Verification" (2000).

32. "Albert de la Chapelle," Wikipedia.

33. Elias et al., "Gender Verification" (2000).

34. A. de la Chapelle, "The Use and Misuse of Sex Chromatin Screening for 'Gender Identification' of Female Athletes," Journal of the American Medical Association (October 10, 1986): 1920–23.

35. M. Genel, "Gender Verification No More?" Medscape Women's Health (May-June 2000), pubmed.org.

36. David Smith, "Report Claims 800m World Champion Caster Semenya Is a Hermaphrodite," The Guardian, September 10, 2009.

37. "IOC Regulations on Female Hyperandrogenism Games of the XXX Olympiad in London," IOC Lausanne, June 22, 2012.

38. "International Olympic Committee: IOC Regulations on Female Hyperandrogenism," Lausanne, June 22, 2012.

39. "Leveling the Playing Field in Female Sport: New Research Published in the British Journal of Sports Medicine," July 27, 2015, IAAF.org.

40. "IAAF Introduces New Eligibility Regulations for Female Classification," April 26, 2018, IAAF.org.

41. Ritchie et al., "Intersex."

42. I.M. Young, "Throwing like a Girl: A Phenomenology of Feminine Body Comportment Motility and Spatiality," Human Studies 3 (1980): 137–156.

43. T. Lewis, "How Men's Brains

Are Wired Differently Than Women's Brains," Life Science (December 2, 2013).

Dora Ratjen

1. "Avery Brundage," Wikipedia.
2. The Unites States Holocaust Memorial Museum, ushmm.org.
3. Dohle, "Het verwoeste."
4. "The Movement to Boycott the Berlin Olympics of 1936," The Unites States Holocaust Memorial Museum, ushmm.org.
5. J.P. O'Malley, "How the Nazis' Token Jew Turned the 1936 Berlin Olympics into a Propaganda Win," The Times of Israel, March 10, 2018, https://www.timesofisrael.com/how-the-nazis-token-jew-turned-the-1936-berlin-olympics-into-a-propaganda-win/.
6. "Hans von Tschammer und Osten," Wikipedia.
7. "The Triumph of Hitler," history-place.com, 2001.
8. H.J. Teichler and S. Felsberg, "Deutsche Sportidolen zwischen Erfolg und Ferfolging pfd," online, 2015.
9. Teichler.
10. Ibid.
11. Leni Riefenstahl, Olympia: Part One, 1938, fragment on YouTube: youtu.be/DX9mc1MC0YY.
12. Kasper Heidelbach (dir.), Berlin '36, 2009.
13. Stephan Berg, "How Dora the Man Competed in the Women's High Jump," Der Spiegel, September 15, 2009, spiegel.de.
14. "Hypospadie," www.patient1.nl/encyclopedie/hypospadie. {URL doesn't work. Title? Author?}
15. Berg.
16. Leni Riefenstahl, Olympia: Part One, 1938, fragment on YouTube: youtu.be/DX9mc1MC0YY.

Foekje Dillema

1. Dohle, "Het verwoeste."
2. Dutch National Record: 24.1 on the 200 meters.
3. Koman.
4. Sylvia Cheeseman, personal interview, March 2008.
5. Henk Weida, personal interview, April 2008.
6. Dohle, "Het verwoeste."
7. Dohle, Max. "Ze zeggen dat ik geen meid ben," Oegstgeest, July 20, 2012.
8. "Het mysterie Foekje Dillema."
9. KNAU minutes, Utrecht, July 8, 1950, unpublished, in the author's collection.
10. Dohle, "Het verwoeste."
11. De Waarheid (newspaper), Amsterdam, July 14, 1950.
12. Aafke Dillema, personal interviews, June 2005–January 2008.
13. H. Dillema, personal interview, March 2008.
14. Dohle, "Het verwoeste."
15. Geesje Jorna, personal interview, August 10, 2007.
16. Lynne Emery, "An Examination of the 1928 Olympic 800 Meter Race for Women," Proceedings of the North American Society for Sport 30, 1982 (pdf).
17. "Het mysterie Foekje Dillema."
18. Klaas Peerenboom, personal interview, February 12, 2008.
19. Geesje Jorna, personal interview, August 21, 2007.
20. Joukje de Fries, personal interview, November 12, 2018.
21. Koman.
22. Aad Heere and Bart Kappenburg, 130 jaar Athletiek in Nederland, 1870–2000. (Koninklijke Nederlandse Atletiek Unie, Nieuwegein, 2000).
23. Stichting Atletiekerfgoed, atletiekerfgoed.nl.

24. Heere and Kappenburg.
25. Klaas Peerenboom, personal interview, March 12, 2008.
26. Dohle, "Het verwoeste."
27. "Tollien Schuurman," Wikipedia.
28. Dohle, "Het verwoeste."
29. Sylvia Cheeseman, personal interviews, March 2008.
30. "Foekje Dilemma," isgeschiedenis.nl.
31. "Het mysterie Foekje Dillema."
32. Ibid.
33. Dohle, "Ze zeggen dat ik geen meid ben."
34. "Leveling the Playing Field in Female Sport."

Ewa Klobukowska

1. Kay Schaffer and Sidonie Smith, The Olympics at the Millennium: Power, Politics, and the Games (New Brunswick, NJ: Rutgers University Press, 2000).
2. "Ewa Kłobukowska," https://pl.m.wikipedia.org/wiki/Ewa_Kłobukowska (Polish wiki).
3. Stefan Wiederkehr, "Unser Mädchen sind alle Einwandfrei; die Klobukowska affaire von 1967 in zeitgenössige press," 2007.
4. "Soviet Union: The Olympic Games," Wikipedia.
5. Max Dohle, "De vergeten competitie," NRC Handelsblad, January 10, 2007.
6. Schaffer and Smith.
7. "Track's Most Resilient (and Suspect) Record Is in Danger," The New York Times, June 15, 2017.
8. Schaffer and Smith.
9. The syndrome is congenital adrenal hyperplasia.
10. Schaffer and Smith.
11. "Genetics: Mosaic in X & Y," Time magazine, September 29, 1967.

12. Franco Barberis, "Tschutti: Wen die Biologie..." Sport, 1967.
13. "Who Goes There?" Newsweek, September 25, 1967.
14. "Die blonde Polin Eva Klobukowska (21) wurde zum Adam," Blick, September 16, 1967.
15. X0 is also a theoretic possibility. But she wouldn't have been banned after further examination.
16. Guy Adams, "Tarnished Gold: Some of the Great Olympics cheats," The Independent, August 1, 2012.
17. For this biography I read several Polish sources via Google translate. "Ewa Klobukowska" (Nieznana Historia); "Falszywe Oskarzenia Zlamany Jej Kariere" (Styl); "Ewa Kłobukowska usłyszała: nie jest pani kobietą!" (kobieta); "Ewa Kłobukowska—skrzywdzona mistrzyni" (Muzeum Histoi Polski).
18. "Records of Polish Girl Sprinter Who Flunked Sex Test Barred," New York Times, February 26, 1968.
19. Simon Jenkins, Sport Science Handbook (Multi-Science Publishing, 2005).

Erika Schinegger

1. M. Hendrick, "Is It a Boy or a Girl?" Johns Hopkins Magazine (1993).
2. Sarah Creighton and Catherine Minto, "Managing Intersex: Most Vaginal Surgery in Childhood Should Be Deferred," British Medical Journal (December 1, 2001).
3. "David Reimer," Wikipedia.
4. Kurt Mayer (dir.), Erik(a): Der Mann der Weltmeisterin wurde. Vienna, 2005.
5. "Huwelijk tussen neef en nicht moet kunnen," Algemeen Dagblad, ANP/Rdactie, July 12, 2011.
6. See chapter on Maria Patiño.

Chapter Notes

Stella Walsh

1. Rob Tannenbaum, "The Life and Murder of Stella Walsh, Intersex Olympic Champion," Olympic Longread, Longreads.com, August 2016.
2. Matt Tullis, "Who Was Stella Walsh? The Story of the Intersex Olympian," Sbnation.com, June 27, 2013.
3. Sharon Kinny-Hanson, The Life of Helen Stephens: The Fulton Flash (Southern Illinois University Press, 2004).
4. Mike Olszewski and Janice Olszewski, Cleveland TV Tales: Stories from the Golden Age of Local Television (Gray & Company, Publishers, 2014).
5. "Athletics at the 1932 Summer Olympics—Women's 100 Meters," Wikipedia.
6. "Stanisława Walasiewicz," Wikipedia.
7. Kinny-Hanson.
8. Guy Walters, Berlin Games: How Hitler Stole the Olympic Dream (reprint; Harper Perennial, 2007).
9. Kinny-Hanson.
10. "Coroner's Report Says Stella Walsh 'lived and died' a Woman," UPI, February 11, 1981.
11. Victor Cohn, "Stella Walsh Found by Coroner to Have Mainly Male Genes," Washington Post, February 13, 1981.

Maria José Martinez Patiño

1. A. de la Chapelle, "The Use and Misuse of Sex Chromatin Screening for 'Gender Identification' of Female Athletes," Journal of the American Medical Association (October 10, 1986): 1920–23.
2. Elias et al. (2000).
3. J.L. Simpson et al., "Gender Verification in the Olympics," JAMA 84, 12 (September 27, 2000): 1568–1569.
4. Maria Martinez Patiño, "Personal Account: A Woman Tried and Tested," The Lancet 366 (December 2005): S38.
5. CAS, Dutee Chand vs. Athletics Federation of India (AFI) and the International Association of Athletics Federations (IAAF), interim arbitral award delivered by the Court of Arbitration for Sport. Tas-cas.org, 2014.
6. Elias et al. (2000).
7. Elias et al. (2000).

Blackmail and Suicide

1. Pilavullakandi Thekkeparambil Usha is her full name.
2. "Pilavullakandi Thekkeparambil Usta," Wikipedia.
3. Nihal Koshie, "The Rising Star Who Ended Her Life Much Before Dutee Chand Challenged the Rules," Indian Express, September 9, 2018.
4. Mayabhushan Nagvenkar, "Pratima Gaonkar: Driven to Suicide by Media and State Apathy. How Many of Us Remember Her?" Newslaundry.com, July 21, 2012.
5. Sandesh Prabhudesai, "Coach Transferred Following Athlete's Suicide," Rediff.com, November 9, 2001.
6. Mitra Dola, "I Am a Female. I Once Loved a Man," Outlook India, July 30, 2012.
7. There was also a female athlete diagnosed with 5 alpha reductase deficiency. See Wikipedia for details on this condition.
8. Elias et al. (2002).
9. "Gender Controversy: Run Pinki Run!" Times of India, June 20, 2012.
10. Soutik Biwas, "The Degradation of Pinki Pramanik," BBC News India, July 4, 2012.
11. Biwas.
12. "Pinki Pramanik Blames Injections for Her 'Masculine' Physique," India Today, July 24, 2014.

162

13. Read the last chapter of this book.

14. Biwas.

15. "Pinki Asks for Police Protection," The Hindu, July 2012.

16. S. Bhanbani, "Pinki Is Not a Female, Claims Expert after Test," Mail Online India, July 13, 2012.

17. "Medical Experts Doubt Pinki Pramanik Can Rape," Times of India, November 15, 2013, timesofindia.indiatimes.com.

18. "Pinki Pramanik," Wikipedia.

19. "Nine Months After Clearing Rape Taint, Pinki Pramanik Battles to Get Back on Track," The Indian Express, July 6, 2015.

20. "Santhi Soundarajan," Wikipedia.

21. "The Sad Story of India's Santhi Soundarajan," China Daily, October 1, 2007. chinadaily.com.cn.

22. "Indian Athlete Fails Gender Test," BBC News, December 18, 2006.

23. "Caught in the Middle," ESPN, August 1, 2013.

24. "The Humiliating Practice of Sex Testing Female Athletes," New York Times Magazine, July 2016.

25. "Santhi Turns to Coaching after Suicide Bid," Reuters, June 2009.

26. "The Travails of Santhi Soundarajan," Fountain Ink Magazine, August 6, 2016, https://m.youtube.com/watch?v=63hDLndWmqU.

27. "Santhi Soundarajan," Wikipedia.

28. "The Humiliating Practice of Sex Testing Female Athletes."

29. "Santhi Soundarajan," Wikipedia.

Sarah Gronert

1. "Intersex Society of North America," National Post, January 27, 2017.

2. Aaron Hicklin, "Intersex and Proud: Model Hanne Gaby Odiele on Finally Celebrating Her Body," The Guardian, April 23, 2017.

3. Ibid.

4. 10 nanomoles per liter of blood.

5. Roger I. Abrams, Sports Justice: The Law and the Business of Sports (Boston: Northeastern University Press, 2010).

6. Ibid.

7. "IOC Rules Transgender Athletes Can Take Part in Olympics without Surgery," The Guardian, January 25, 2016.

8. www.ioc.org.

9. "IOC Relaxes Guidelines on Transgender Athletes: Surgical Anatomical Changes as a Precondition to Participation Is Not Necessary," The Associated Press, January 24, 2016.

Caster Semenya and Dutee Chand

1. "What Is Hermaphrodite in Pedi?" IOL News, October 2, 2009.

2. William Lee Adams, "Could This Women's World Champ Be a Man?" Time, August 21, 2009.

3. Anna Kessel, "The Unequal Battle: Privilege, Genes, Gender and Power," The Guardian, February 18, 2018.

4. "Atlete Semenya moet medicatie nemen om bij vrouwen actief te mogen blijven," April 26, 2018, Nu.nl.

5. "50 People That Matter 2010: 50. Caster Semenya," New Statesman, September 27, 2010.

6. "Traumatized Semenya Skips Exams," BBC News, October 15, 2009.

7. Simon Hart, "Caster Semenya 'is a hermaphrodite,' Tests Show," Sydney Daily Telegraph, September 9, 2009.

8. "Complaint Filed in Semenya's Case," The New York Times, September 15, 2009.

9. "South African Official Lied about Semenya Gender Tests," CNN, September 22, 2009.

10. See the Interim Arbitral Award of the CAS, in the case of Chand vs. the IAAF, discussed later in this chapter.

11. "New IAAF Testosterone Rules Could Slow Caster Semenya by up to Seven Seconds," The Guardian, April 26, 2018.

12. Peter Sonken, et al., "Medical and Ethical Concerns Regarding Women with Hyperandrogenism and Elite Sport," The Journal of Clinical Endocrinology (2013).

13. "Verdere verbetering anticonceptiepil door herstel testosteronspiegel," January 8, 2014, umcutrecht.nl.

14. A reference to Santhi Soundarajan.

15. Ruth Pawader, "Indian Dutee Chand, Set to Run in the Olympics, Has Been Humiliated by Sex-Testing," Sydney Morning Herald, July 15, 2018.

16. "Fighting the Body She Was Born With," New York Times, October 2014.

17. Shreedutta Chidananda, "Dutee Chand Finds Support in Santhi," The Hindu, July 19, 2014.

18. Dutee Chand vs. Athletic Federation of India and the International Association of Athletic Federations. Interim Arbitral Award delivered by the Court of Arbitration for Sport, tas-cas.org, 2104.

19. Christie Blatchford, "Female Athletes Competing Against 'Intersex' Women a Difficult, Complex Issue," National Post, August 21, 2016.

20. S. Bermon and P. Garnier, "Serum Androgen Levels and Their Relation to Performance in Track and Field: Mass Spectrometry Results from 2127 Observations in Male and Female Elite Athletes," British Journal of Sports Medicine (September 5, 2017): 1309–1314.

21. Eline Van Suchtelen, "Zonder hormoonremmers vindt IAAf Caster Semenya een man," Trouw, May 9, 2018.

22. Andy Bull, "IAAF Accused of 'blatant racism' over New Testosterone Level Regulations," The Guardian, April 28, 2018.

23. "Did Flawed Data Lead Track Astray on Testosterone in Women?" New York Times, July 12, 2018.

24. "Caster Semenya: IAAF to Respect CAS Decision on Testosterone Rules," BBC, June 27, 2018.

Bibliography

Abrams, Roger I. *Sports Justice: The Law and the Business of Sports.* Boston: Northeastern University Press, 2010.

Adams, Guy. "Tarnished Gold: Some of the Great Olympics Cheats." *The Independent*, August 1, 2012.

Adams, William Lee. "Could This Women's World Champ Be a Man?" *Time*, August 21, 2009.

"Alice Milliat." Wikipedia.

"Athletics at the 1932 Summer Olympics—Women's 100 Meters." Wikipedia.

"Atlete Semenya moet medicatie nemen om bij vrouwen actief te mogen blijven." April 26, 2018. nu.nl.

"Avery Brundage." Wikipedia.

Ballantyne, Kay, Manfred Kaye, et al. "Sex and Gender Issues in Competitive Sports: Investigation of a Historical Case Leads to a New Viewpoint." *British Journal of Sports Medicine* vol. 46, issue 8 (June 2012). Bjsm.bjm.com.

Barberis, Franco. "Tschutti: Wen die Biologie…" *Sport* (1967).

Berg, Stephan. "How Dora the Man Competed in the Women's High Jump." *Der Spiegel,* September 15, 2009, spiegel.de.

Bermon, S., and P. Garnier. "Serum Androgen Levels and Their Relation to Performance in Track and Field: Mass Spectrometry Results from 2127 Observations in Male and Female Elite Athletes." *British Journal of Sports Medicine* (September 5, 2017): 1309–1314.

Bermon, Stéphane, et al. "Women with Hyperandrogism in Elite Sports: Scientific and Ethical Rationales for Regulating." *The Journal of Clinical Endocrinology and Metabolism,* vol. 100, issue 3 (March 2015). Academic. oup.com.

Bhanbani, S. "Pinki Is Not a Female, Claims Expert after Test." *Mail Online India*, July 13, 2012.

Biwas, Soutik. "The Degradation of Pinki Pramanik." *BBC News India,* July 4, 2012.

"Het bizarre leven van Violette Morris: autocoureur, travestiet en nazibeul." *Het Nieuwsblad.* January 11, 2017.

Blatchford, Christie. "Female Athletes Compcting Against 'Intersex' Women a Difficult, Complex Issue." *National Post*, August 21, 2016.

Bosley Ziegler, John. NIDA Research Monograph Index, Wikipedia, 1990.

Brown, Oliver. "The Person Who Pays for Everything Is the Athlete." Telegraph.co.uk. November 14, 2016.

Bull, Andy. "IAAF Accused of 'blatant racism' over New Testosterone Level Regulations." *The Guardian,* April 28, 2018.

Cahn, Susan. *Coming On Strong: Gender and Sexuality in 20th-Century Women's Sports.* Cambridge: Harvard University Press, 1995.

Bibliography

"Caster Semenya: IAAF to Respect CAS Decision on Testosterone Rules." BBC, June 27, 2018.

"Caught in the Middle." ESPN, August 1, 2013.

Chidananda, Shreedutta. "Dutee Chand Finds Support in Santhi." *The Hindu*, July 19, 2014.

Cohn, Victor. "Stella Walsh Found by Coroner to Have Mainly Male Genes." *Washington Post*, February 13, 1981.

"Complaint Filed in Semenya's Case." *The New York Times*, September 15, 2009.

"Coroner's Report Says Stella Walsh 'lived and died' a Woman." UPI, February 11, 1981.

Creighton, Sarah, and Catherine Minto. "Managing Intersex: Most Vaginal Surgery in Childhood Should Be Deferred." *British Medical Journal* (December 1, 2001).

"David Reimer." Wikipedia.

De la Chapelle, A. "The Use and Misuse of Sex Chromatin Screening for 'Gender Identification' of Female Athletes," *Journal of the American Medical Association* (October 10, 1986): 1920–23.

"Did Flawed Data Lead Track Astray on Testosterone in Women?" *New York Times*, July 12, 2018.

"Die blonde Polin Eva Klobukowska (21) wurde zum Adam." *Blick*, September 16, 1967.

Dohle, Max. "Het verwoeste leven van Foekje Dilema: de grootste tragedie uit de Nederlandse sportgeschiedenis." *Arbeiderspers* (Amsterdam), 2008.

Dohle, Max, "De vergeten competitie." *NRC Handelsblad,* January 10, 2007.

Dohle, Max. "Ze zeggen dat ik geen meid ben." *Oegstgeest*, July 20, 2012.

"Dokument Ramm: Erkjennelsen." https://youtu.be/ehnMEjHyIgM.

Dola, Mitra. "I Am a Female. I Once Loved a Man." *Outlook India,* July 30, 2012.

Elias, L., Arne Ljungqvist et al. "Gender Verification of Female Athletes." *Genetics in Medicine* (2000): 249–254.

Elias, L., Arne Ljungqvist et al. "Gender Verification of Female Athletes." *Genet Med* (July-August 2002). www.ncbi.nlm.nih.gov.

Emery, Lynne. "An Examination of the 1928 Olympic 800 Meter Race for Women. Proceedings of the North American Society for Sport 30, 1982 (pdf).

"Ewa Kłobukowska." https://pl.m.wikipedia.org/wiki/Ewa_Kłobukowska (Polish wiki).

"50 People That Matter 2010: 50. Caster Semenya." *New Statesman,* September 27, 2010.

"Foekje Dilemma." Isgeschiedenis.nl.

"Gender Controversy: Run Pinki Run!" *Times of India,* June 20, 2012.

"Gender Verification in Sports." Wikipedia.

Genel, M. "Gender Verification No More?" *Medscape Women's Health* (May-June 2000). pubmed.org.

"Genetics: Mosaic in X & Y." *Time* magazine, September 29, 1967.

"Girl Changes into Man." *Your Body*, August 1936.

Guttman, Allen. *The Olympics: A History of the Modern Games.* Google Books, 1992.

Hannah-Shmouni, Fady, et al. "Revisiting the Prevalence of Nonclassic Congenital Adrenal Hyperplasia in U.S. Ashkenazi Jews and Caucasians." *Genetics in Medicine* (November 19, 2017). Pubmed.com.

"Hans von Tschammer und Osten." Wikipedia.

Hargreaves, J. and E. Anderson. *Routledge *International Handbook of Sport, Gender and Sexuality.* Routledge, 2014.

"Harry Klinefelter." Wikipedia.

Hart, Simon. "Caster Semenya 'is a hermaphrodite,' Tests Show." *Sydney Daily Telegraph*, September 9, 2009.

Heere, Aad, and Bart Kappenburg. *130 jaar Athletiek in Nederland, 1870–2000.* Koninklijke Nederlandse Atletiek Unie, Nieuwegein, 2000.

Heggie, Vanessa. "The H Word: Sex Testing and the Olympics: Myths, Rumours and Confirmation Bias." guardian.com. August 2, 2012.

Heggie, Vanessa. "Testing Sex and Gender in Sports: Reinventing, Reimagining and Reconstructing Histories." *Endeavour* 34, 4 (December 2010): 157–163.

Heidelbach, Kasper (dir.). Berlin '36. 2009.

Hendrick, M. "Is It a Boy or a Girl?" *Johns Hopkins Magazine* (1993).

Hicklin, Aaron. "Intersex and Proud: Model Hanne Gaby Odiele on Finally Celebrating Her Body." *The Guardian,* April 23, 2017.

"History for All: The History of Women's Football." TheFA.com, undated.

"Homosexuality in Association Football." Wikipedia.

"How Common Is Intersex?" Intersex Society of North America. www.isna.org.

"The Humiliating Practice of Sex Testing Female Athletes." *Times Magazine,* July 2016.

"Huwelijk tussen neef en nicht moet kunnen." *Algemeen Dagblad, ANP/ Redactie,* July 12, 2011.

"Hypospadie." www.patient1.nl/encyclopedie/hypospadie.

"IAAF Introduces New Eligibility Regulations for Female Classification." 2018. www.iaaf.org.

"Indian Athlete Fails Gender Test." *BBC News*, December 18, 2006.

"International Olympic Committee: IOC Regulations on Female Hyperandrogenism." Lausanne, June 22, 2012.

"Intersex Society of North America." *National Post*, January 27, 2017.

"IOC Regulations on Female Hyperandrogenism Games of the XXX Olympiad in London." IOC Lausanne, June 22, 2012.

"IOC Relaxes Guidelines on Transgender Athletes: Surgical Anatomical Changes as a Precondition to Participation Is Not Necessary." The Associated Press, January 24, 2016.

"IOC Rules Transgender Athletes Can Take Part in Olympics without Surgery." *The Guardian*, January 25, 2016.

"Irina Press." Wikipedia.

"Is Athletic Performance Determined by Genetics?" U.S. National Library of Genetics. Undated. ghr.nlm.nih.gov.

Jacobs, P.A., and J.A. Strong. "A Case of Human Intersexuality Having a Possible XXY Sex-Determining Mechanism." January 31, 1959. pubmed.com.

Jenkins, Simon. *Sport Science Handbook.* Multi-Science Publishing, 2005.

Kessel, Anna. "The Unequal Battle: Privilege, Genes, Gender and Power." *The Guardian*, February 18, 2018.

Kidd, Bruce, and Cesar Torres. *Historicizing the Pan-American Games.* Routledge, 2015.

Kinny-Hanson, Sharon. *The Life of Helen Stephens: The Fulton Flash.* Southern Illinois University Press, 2004.

Klumper, Frans. Personal interview. September 21, 2016.

KNAU minutes, Utrecht, July 8, 1950. Unpublished, in the author's collection.

Bibliography

Kolota, Gina. "I.O.C. Panel Calls for Treatment in Sex Ambiguity Cases." *New York Times*, January 20, 2010.

Koman, K. *Een koningin met mannen-benen: Fanny Blankers-Koen atlete van de eeuw.* Amsterdam: Dedico Grave, 2003.

Koshie, Nihal. "The Rising Star Who Ended Her Life Much Before Dutee Chand Challenged the Rules." *Indian Express*, September 9, 2018.

"Leveling the Playing Field in Female Sport: New Research Published in the *British Journal of Sports Medicine.*" July 27, 2015. IAAF.org.

Lewis, Denise. "Semenya Will Top the Podium—Yet She Can Never Win." *Telegraph*, August 16, 2016.

Lewis, T. "How Men's Brains Are Wired Differently Than Women's Brains." *Life Science* (December 2, 2013).

"Lily Parr." Wikipedia.

Martinez Patiño, Maria. "Personal Account: A Woman Tried and Tested." *The Lancet* 366 (2005): S38.

Mayer, Kurt (dir.). *Erik(a): Der Mann der Weltmeisterin wurde.* Vienna, 2005.

Mededeling Nederlandsch Tijdschrift voor Geneeskunde, 1936.

"Medical Experts Doubt Pinki Pramanik Can Rape." *Times of India,* November 15, 2013. timesofindia.indiatimes.com.

"Medicine. Change of Sex." *Time* magazine, August 24, 1936.

"The Movement to Boycott the Berlin Olympics of 1936." The Unites States Memorial Holocaust Museum, ushmm.org.

"Het mysterie Foekje Dillema." Andere Tijden Sport VPRO Hilversum, July 6, 2008.

Nagvenkar, Mayabhushan. "Goa's Pinki Praminik." Newslaundry.com. July 21, 2012.

Nagvenkar, Mayabhushan. "Pratima Gaonkar: Driven to Suicide by Media and State Apathy. How Many of Us Remember Her?" Newslaundry.com, July 21, 2012.

"New IAAF Testosterone Rules Could Slow Caster Semenya by up to Seven Seconds." *The Guardian*, April 26, 2018.

"Nine Months After Clearing Rape Taint, Pinki Pramanik Battles to Get Back on Track." *The Indian Express*, July 6, 2015.

Olszewski, Mike, and Janice Olszewski. *Cleveland TV Tales: Stories from the Golden Age of Local Television.* Gray & Company, Publishers, 2014.

O'Malley, J.P. "How the Nazis' Token Jew Turned the 1936 Berlin Olympics into a Propaganda Win." *The Times of Israel*, March 10, 2018. https://www.timesofisrael.com/how-the-nazis-token-jew-turned-the-1936-berlin-olympics-into-a-propaganda-win/.

Padawer, Ruth. "The Humiliating Practice of Sex Testing Female Athletes." *New York Times Magazine,* June 28, 2016.

Padawer, Ruth. "Indian Dutee Chand, Set to Run in the Olympics, Has Been Humiliated by Sex-Testing." *Sydney Morning Herald*, July 15, 2018.

"Pilavullakandi Thekkeparambil Usta." Wikipedia.

"Pinki Asks for Police Protection." *The Hindu*, July 2012.

"Pinki Pramanik." Wikipedia.

"Pinki Pramanik Blames Injections for Her 'Masculine' Physique." *India Today*, July 24, 2014.

Prabhudesai, Sandesh. "Coach Transferred Following Athlete's Suicide." Rediff.com, November 9, 2001.

"Records of Polish Girl Sprinter Who Flunked Sex Test Barred." *New York Times,* February 26, 1968.

Riefenstahl, Leni. *Olympia Fest der Völker*. Berlin, 1938.

Riefenstahl, Leni. *Olympia: Part One*. 1938. YouTube (fragment): https://youtu.be/DX9mc1MC0YY.

Ritchie, Robert, et al. "Intersex and the Olympic Games." *Journal of the Royal Society of Medicine* (August 1, 2008).

"The Sad Story of India's Santhi Soundarajan." *China Daily*, October 1, 2007. chinadaily.com.cn.

"Santhi Soundarajan." Wikipedia.

"Santhi Turns to Coaching after Suicide Bid." Reuters, June 2009.

Schaffer, Kay, and Sidonie Smith. *The Olympics at the Millennium: Power, Politics, and the Games*. New Brunswick, NJ: Rutgers University Press, 2000.

Schultz, Jaime. *Qualifying Times: Points of Change in U.S. Women Sport*. Urbana: University of Illinois Press, 2014.

Sebba, Anne. *Les Parisiennes: How the Women of Paris Lived, Loved and Died under Nazi Occupation*. St. Martin's Press, 2016.

Simpson, J.L., et al. "Gender Verification in the Olympics." *JAMA* 84, 12 (September 27, 2000): 1568–1569.

Smith, David. "Report Claims 800m World Champion Caster Semenya Is a Hermaphrodite." *The Guardian*, September 10, 2009.

"So What If Some Olympian Females Have High Levels of Testosterone?" Theconversation.com. August 15, 2016.

Sonken, Peter, et al. "Medical and Ethical Concerns Regarding Women with Hyperandrogenism and Elite Sport." *The Journal of Clinical Endocrinology* (2013).

"South African Official Lied about Semenya Gender Tests." CNN, September 22, 2009.

"Soviet Union: The Olympic Games." Wikipedia.

Stichting Atletiekerfgoed, atletiekerfgoed.nl.

Szabo, Gabriela. "True Romania." Surprisingromania.blogspot.com.

"Tamara Press." Wikipedia.

Tannenbaum, Rob. "The Life and Murder of Stella Walsh, Intersex Olympic Champion." Olympic Longread, Longreads.com. August 2016.

Tebbutt, Clare. "The Spectre of the 'Man-Woman Athlete': Mark Weston, Zdenek Koubek, the 1936 Olympics and the Uncertainty of Sex." *Woman's History Review*, 24.5 (2015): 721–738.

Teichler, H.J., and S. Felsberg. "Deutsche Sportidolen zwischen Erfolg und Ferfolging pfd." Online, 2015.

"Tollien Schuurman." Wikipedia.

"Track's Most Resilient (and Suspect) Record Is in Danger." *The New York Times*, June 15, 2017.

"Traumatized Semenya Skips Exams." *BBC News*, October 15, 2009.

"The Travails of Santhi Soundarajan." Fountain Ink Magazine, August 6, 2016. https://m.youtube.com/watch?v=63hDLndWmqU.

"The Triumph of Hitler." History Place, 2001. historyplace.com.

Tullis, Matt. "Who Was Stella Walsh? The Story of the Intersex Olympian." Sbnation.com. June 27, 2013.

Van Suchtelen, Eline. "Zonder hormoonremmers vindt IAAf Caster Semenya een man." *Trouw*, May 9, 2018.

Velthuis, Rob. "Is Semenya vrouw genoeg om aan de Spelen mee te mogen doen?" *Dagblad Trouw & Nieuwsblad*, August 18, 2016.

"Verdere verbetering anticonceptiepil door herstel testosteronspiegel," January 8, 2014. umcutrecht.nl.

Walters, Guy. *Berlin Games: How Hitler*

Bibliography

Stole the Olympic Dream. Reprint; Harper Perennial, 2007.

Walters, Guy. *Berlin 1936: How Hitler Stole the Olympian Dream.* London, 2006.

"What Is Hermaphrodite in Pedi?" *IOL News*, October 2, 2009.

"Who Goes There?" *Newsweek,* September 25, 1967.

"Witold Smętek." Wikipedia.

"Women's World Games 1934." Wikipedia.

"World Games Athletics." Wikipedia.

Young, I.M. "Throwing Like a Girl: A Phenomenology of Feminine Body Comportment Motility and Spatiality." *Human Studies* 3 (1980): 137–156.

Zeigler, Cyd. "18 Out LGBT Participants in the Women's World Cup." Outsports.com, May 31, 2015.

Interviews

Aad, Heere. May 2007.

Cheeseman, Sylvia. March 2008.

de Fries, Joukje. November 12, 2018.

Dillema, Aafke. June 2005–January 2008.

Dillema, H. March 2008.

Jorna, Geesje. August 10 and 21, 2007.

Klumper, Frans. September 21, 2016.

Peerenboom, Klaas. February 12 and March 12, 2008.

van Gennip, Yvonne. November 2010.

Weida, Henk. April 2008.

Index

Index

Index

www.ingramcontent.com/pod-product-compliance
Lightning Source LLC
Chambersburg PA
CBHW031136270326
41929CB00011B/1649